Eloise

Loving a
Sociopath

Catherine Lockwood

For Jes and Faye

Table of contents

Prologue

She came into my world and then swiftly blew away. With an empty, aching heart, I must stand alone today. A single tear upon my cheek feels cold against the breeze. All the sounds around me are crying Eloise.

July 22nd 2013 – Pandora

It rained hard on the day of Eloise's funeral. She would have hated that. She always said that funerals should only take place on sunny days. She said that sunshine was a sign of happiness and celebration and rainy days were a sign of something more sinister. She was a funny little thing, but there was some wisdom in those words. There was no sun and that was what triggered my tears. None of her favourite songs were played and the whole occasion was too sombre – a fiasco – and they thought they knew her. She once told me she would like the first song to be *Hurt* by Christina Aguilera, to remind them of how badly she was treated and how it was too late for them to say sorry. She also wanted her favourite Hymn, Jerusalem to be sung, but that was her contrary way. The clergy believe that Jerusalem is unfitting for funerals and she knew that full well. She also wanted The Laughing Policeman to be played as the coffin was carried to the cemetery.

"That'll put a smile on their stupid faces," she said, laughing her wicked, dirty laugh.

I remained silent because only Jude and I knew what Eloise would have wanted ... she only ever spoke of such things to us. She died on her forty-fifth birthday and that was no coincidence. The torment was too much for me to bear. Soon I would have to tell someone what had happened. It felt as though I was protecting Jude rather than Eloise which angered me because I hated him with a passion. He had undone everything she had achieved in such a short time. Her child and ex-husband were grey with despair. They knew something of Jude and were forever suspicious of her *other* life – but Eloise had sworn me to secrecy.

Andy lurked in the background beside some trees and no one seemed to notice him – except for me. We had never met although I knew it was him. He held a rose and wept. A sudden chill tore through my body. There were things I would have to tell him too.

Perhaps Eloise somehow knew she was in danger. Months before her death, she had given me the key to her desk. It was filled with diaries she had kept religiously since the 1980's. There was also a rough draft of her new novel that, in keeping with her writing style, was based on her journals and the people she knew. She made me promise to divulge nothing about the true extent of the affair – unless anything untoward were to happen before she had time to finish her books. She was forever the drama queen, but this time I sensed fear behind those laughing eyes. She tried to make light of it as she discerned my angst. I saw very little of her after that...

The clues were indeed in her work and I had been right about Jude. It was my job to unearth the events following her final journal entry. If she had liberty to live without secrets, none of this would have happened. I kept my word however and her family's *deserved* bewilderment would continue – at least for a while.

Childhood

My name is Pandora and I have lost my best friend.

We met at secondary school when we were eleven years old. There was an instant affinity between us which would last for over more than three decades. Eloise was off the wall and uninhibited with no inner monologue, which would often make for utter chaos. We would laugh all day at school and learned very little. We were eerily like-minded but quite different to look at. Eloise was petite with a mop of strawberry-blond hair, hiding a pretty face. She was a tomboy and people remarked that she looked like one of those trolls you put on the end of your pencil. I was more of a girly-girl with dark hair, plenty of curves and a slightly more feminine sense of dress.

When she was fourteen, Eloise forgot her fountain pen at school one day. Our English teacher, Mrs. Halibut, who was always infuriated with our silliness, told Eloise to find something to write with or stand outside the classroom. Eloise promptly lifted her bosom from her bra and dipped her nipple into the ink-well. (It was lucky that we attended a school for girls.) She was quickly thrown out of the classroom, tucking her boob back into her shirt as she went. Another time, she skipped PE so the teacher told her to have a shower anyhow by way of a punishment.

"I'm not having a shower; you just want to watch me don't you, you lesbian!"

Truancy was the main occupation in our early teens, as was smoking, singing rather loudly in the middle of shopping centres and occasionally getting drunk on cider.

Eloise was troubled by something or other at home; I think she was sometimes beaten because she would come to school with the most awful bruises. She suffered terrible depression although she hid it well from most. I think I was the only one who knew. Maybe this would account for her behaviour which *even I* sometimes found shocking – but she did make me laugh.

Teens

After leaving school at sixteen, we both went straight to work which was a plenty in those days. Having our own money was wonderful; it gave us the freedom to do as we pleased, in particular getting drunk. All of a sudden we felt very grown up, hanging out in bars and discos. Boys became a big part of our lives and our favourite haunt was a local pub which we visited almost every evening. Eloise loved to drink, as did I, but she was always overly raucous.

Eloise soon fell head-over-heels in love with a boy named Joe, but the relationship failed after a couple of years. Then she met the drunken raucous Jude. He was the most beautiful vision you could ever imagine; tall and handsome with long black hair and the darkest eyes. He was one of those boys that always knew the right thing to say – his chat up lines were unsurpassed. Eloise hung onto his every word and I could see her melting every time he held court. (He loved doing that.) Jude devoured her soul with his appetite for her attention. His emotional issues were so severe that they made Eloise's own appear as slight eccentricities. Jude craved approval and talked about himself constantly, claiming he had never been loved – he always seemed so sorry for himself. His eyes looked empty to me, rather than sad – almost evil. Eloise was sucked in by his hard-luck stories and I was always uneasy about them. After just a few months, Jude left Eloise with a broken heart. I had fully expected this to happen and now it was my job to pick her up again.

All grown up

Eventually we lost touch for a good few years. My career in advertising had taken off well and I moved to London with my partner. Eloise married, had a child and later moved abroad.

Twenty-four years later, we bumped into each other quite by accident. I was living alone after separating from my latest disaster. Eloise had returned to the UK and was unhappy in her own relationship. She was married to a bully, felt trapped, so was desperate to get away from him. Her teenage son, Charlie was hardly any better. He was a good soul and loved her but was brainwashed by his chauvinistic father. They believed that women should only talk of fluffy bunnies or be damned. Eloise had begun to write and her husband just pooh-poohed everything she did, telling her she was stupid. He said that if she ever sold a book he would eat his own head. Our friendship just seemed to resume as if it had never been interrupted. We began to go out regularly and laughed just like we had all those years ago... although Eloise had changed. She was now fairly well adjusted and had obviously worked hard to straighten herself out.

"I don't want my depression to define me," she would say.

Not long after our reunion, Eloise inherited some money from her late parents and separated from her husband. She was sick and tired of his put-downs and controlling ways. She had become fairly strong although I still sensed much insecurity. She asked him to leave and eventually he gave in after much protestation. Her son remained with her but had eyes like a hawk and told her she must never have a boyfriend. Eloise thought she had tired of men and just laughed it off, telling him not to worry. She was happy to be emotionally and financially independent at last.

***

Facebook was all the rage and we decided to try and look up our old friends of some thirty years ago. Eloise turned up on my doorstep one afternoon and her face had a glow about it which took years off her.

"You'll never guess who I found on Facebook?"

"Go on ... tell me."

"Jude!"

"Fucking hell! How, where, when?"

"Well, I went on the 'Who used to live in Hampton' page and saw him posting. Then I messaged him and asked if he was the Jude I once knew. He looked a lot different in his photos, but those eyes! The eyes never change do they? He has short pepper and salt hair but it is him."

"Are you sure?"

"Yes it is. I friend requested and messaged him and he answered."

"What did he say?"

"He was a bit cheeky actually and used a hint of saucy innuendo – nothing changed there then. He was nice though. He writes novels for children now and has published his memoirs. He's really turned his life around."

"I should bloody hope so, he was off his rocker. Are you sure you want to go there again?"

"Yes, he's very different now – seems so calm. I think its kismet. We both had loads of problems and have sorted ourselves out now. He writes too, which is the weirdest thing and he seems really interested in me."

***

There began Eloise and Jude's intense online relationship which eventually led to their meeting again... In the beginning, Eloise would excitedly update me about their romance at the end of each day. She would even forward me some of the emails and messages he had sent her. Most of them were silliness and larks although some were so impassioned; one might believe they were deeply in love. It felt as though I had shared their every intimate thought which often made me uncomfortable. I had been bound unwittingly into voyeurism – or at least that was how it felt. We would still meet up from time to time, but Jude was now the centre of her world and all she talked of with her usual poetic recount – and his, which was often added to the mix. I would sometimes escape into the kitchen to roll my eyes where I could still hear her twittering on. The whole affair was rather odd and still not consummated after many weeks, although they had been fully sexually active during their teens. They called themselves Cathy and Heathcliff and it all seemed rather sweet until the rot set in. The next year would prove to be the hardest challenge for Eloise and I would lose her to a closeted world of deceit.

Chapter 1
"It's written in the stars"

April 2nd 2012

This new chapter in my life has made me happier than I ever imagined. Just being in touch with Jude again seems to take away all my fears and depression. There is an excitement in my soul that I honestly thought I would never feel again. We speak every day now; several times in fact, and I feel like a teenager jumping with joy each time I receive a message, text or call. We actually spoke for the first time on Friday and at first I thought he had a funny voice – a slight impediment with his R's. I had forgotten what he sounded like and it made me cringe a bit to begin with. He says years in a very peculiar fashion – it sounds like yarrrrrs – almost how a very posh person would say it. We are meeting for the first time in 'yarrrrrs' next week and I cannot even begin to describe my excitement. It is very frightening however, and my emotions are all over the place. I am older now and will have to do a few exercises. How can I get rid of these bingo wings and my belly in five days? My roots need doing too... Oh bloody hell!

Today we met yayyyyyy! After all those years, nothing had changed all that much. Jude remains very witty and charming and seemingly without the neurosis of 1986 – thank goodness. He is still quite deep in his conversation and talks a lot about his unhappy childhood but I think he has moved on. He has grown into an extremely handsome man – no longer a wild-haired hippy, rather more of a fetching George Clooney type. The beautiful eyes and even more beautiful smile continue to radiate his lovely face. We ate fresh salmon and salad as we chatted – it felt so comfortable and right. It was meant to be – I am sure, and although I feel rather insecure about my older face and body, there was an instant attraction – I could feel it. Jude walked me to my car and softly kissed me on the cheek.

There was no awkwardness at all and then he took me in his arms and hugged me so hard that I almost fainted with a mixture of joy and my struggle to breathe. I think I love him.

Charlie is going to university next year and I told Jude this would be the perfect time for our relationship to go a stage further. We need to wait until then to go public because it will be easier once I am on my own. Frank, the bastard-bully has always threatened that if I find another man he will batter the pair of us. Jude has reluctantly agreed. He fails to understand the concept of putting children first as he has none of his own. Besides, it could put him in danger, though I refrain from putting a too finer point on that in case it scares him off. There is a sense of some resentment on his part and I do empathise so simply put it down to his naivety.

Jude has never married nor had children, just a string of disastrous relationships and numerous one night stands. He must have had such awful luck in that respect. I am positive that is his reason for his being alone – nothing more sinister I hope. Sometimes people have to wait decades to find their soul-mate – including myself it would seem. I am sure that is all it is.

April 13th

We have just had our second lunch date. This time the conversation moved up a gear woohoo!

"I am so glad to have you back in my world," he said, as he looked into my eyes.

"Do you think we were meant to be, Jude?"

"Definitely, there are so many coincidences in our lives and I don't believe in coincidence, only destiny."

"Will you wait for me until Charlie goes to Uni?"

"Of course I will, darling, we've waited for more than twenty years, another eighteen months won't make any difference. We can have a proper relationship without any distractions and maybe buy a little house in France."

Blimey! We talked much more openly but the proper relationship bit has scared me to death. It took me rather by surprise actually, though at least he's not pushing for sex yet. I wonder what made him come out with such an idea. He seems very keen and is making plans for us already. Why do I find that a bit unsettling? Oh I am just being paranoid. He is very affectionate and absurdly romantic so can melt my heart with a single word.

April 20th

Jude has been sending me poems almost every day, always beginning, 'For Cathy Earnshaw.' When he was young, he resembled the legendary Heathcliff with his long black hair and deep-set dark eyes. He also had Heathcliff's temperament which was menacing at the time. Now he is a nicer Heathcliff; if there is such a thing. Heathcliff is my fantasy man and he knows that … such a clever bugger!

He also sends me the most thoughtful and appropriate love songs by email. Yesterday I received a book through the post – *I wondered why he had asked for my address*. It was a biography of a lady who had lived an unhappy life and had found love in later years. He signed the book with a quote: *'If you love someone let them go. If they come back they will be yours forever. If they don't, then they were never yours in the first place'*… or something like that. He is always so deep and loving; I have never known anything like it.

He lavishes me with gifts, books, art and everything he knows I love. It seems almost *too* perfect. I am falling deeper under his spell by the day and the whole thing is glorious.

Pandora said the other day, "I hope he's not grooming you." I did laugh.

April 24th

Yesterday, I visited Jude's house for the first time after lunch. His house is very Bohemian but incredibly neat. He has two enormous dogs, three guitars and a Wurlitzer in his lounge. We spoke for two hours non-stop without the distractions of a busy restaurant, all the while holding hands. I prayed that he would keep his distance because my lady-garden was rather un-pruned.

"Do you love me, Jude?" I asked, surprising myself and hoping not to sound like a desperate wanton.

"I'll send you a song later by email and you will know how I feel, Cathy."

I love it when he calls me Cathy.

As soon as I walked through my front door, I switched on my laptop. There was an email from Jude ... a song. The anticipation exhilarated me like it did every time I checked my mails. It was 'Only words' by Extreme. I played the song like an excitable toddler, wriggling about, almost failing from my chair. The words sent me into yet another whirlwind of desire. It implied that Jude had no need to say that he loved me; it should be obvious because he had held me tight as though he would never let me go ... just like in the song.

The most endearing thing about our tryst is the sense of humour we share. It is incredible that we laugh at the slightest things like TV shows or just someone walking past his house – sometimes until we cry. When we are together we always hold hands when we talk. Often I sit on Jude's knee at his computer desk as he writes. There is always a sense of teasing in our actions – you could almost describe it as tantric. We often hold each other until a point of ecstasy and then just pull away. It seems to be a mutual, telepathic reaction and I have no idea why it happens, but it is better than any orgasm. Jude always touches me softly as he passes; just a brush of his hand; far enough away from an erogenous area to get away with it. I feel as though I have been numb for the past twenty-five years and sometimes wish we had never been apart. I suppose it was for the best. Now I am fantasising about us living together in his house with our dogs, or even having children together. It has been a long time, but things are coming back to me and I remember just how he had enraptured me before. He has changed for the better but still retains that 'something' that he had all those years ago.

April 27th

The poetry is still coming via me email furiously – I have no idea where he finds the time. He is so talented and makes me wonder if my writing is good enough. Sometimes if he has trouble sleeping, he sits up and writes short stories about us. I check my inbox every morning which invariably contains something magnificent and I am euphoric for the rest of the day. His grammar could do with a bit of a polish but his words are like arrows that softly pierce my heart. He has begun to phone me every afternoon from under his favourite tree in the field where he walks his dogs. He has a strict routine in his daily business which is rather cute; I wish I could be like that. My life is higgledy piggledy and I rarely know what I am going to do next. There is no routine with my writing, except for my journals which I am using for book ideas – and other odds and sods. My house is a shambles and I never make any plans.

It has occurred to me that I always know where Jude is and exactly what he is doing at different stages of the day. This makes our time apart much easier for me because I can envisage everything, so trust him implicitly. There is no mystery about Jude's day-to-day activities. I know everything about them and his ordered little existence – living alone with his dogs. He is safe.

Every morning, I receive a text at 9.30 saying 'good morning, my Cathy.' Then at 11.30, I receive another with four kisses, never any more or any less. He then goes to the gym for half an hour. At noon, I sit by my laptop and wait for his usual email. It normally contains a poem or a love note, saying how much he cares for me and what I mean to his lonely life. At 2 pm he logs onto Facebook and we chat for one hour. At 3 pm he takes his dogs for a walk and texts another four kisses when he arrives at his destination. At 4.30 pm he sits under his favourite tree, eating one apple, one banana and one orange. When he has eaten his fruit, he phones me at 4.45 pm He arrives home at 5.30 pm and logs onto Facebook, where we chat for around thirty minutes. He then watches The Channel Four News and eats toast with honey and peanut butter. At 7pm he has a little sleep on the sofa for about an hour. At 8 pm, he works on a chapter of his current book until 10pm, when he has a break to eat. After his supper, he logs on to Facebook again for another hour long chat with me. At 11pm he watches television for one hour until his bed-time at midnight. At 12.30 am he texts me goodnight. God forbid I ever nod off and miss anything – he will always think the worst. It is fucking exhausting at times, but hey-ho!

<h2 style="text-align:center">April 30th</h2>

Jude is a bit of a sulker at times and it is always over the most unimportant things. He has down moments and complains if I am not feeling his mood. It upsets me but we are still getting to know each other and nobody is perfect. Frank made me doubt myself and I swear this will never happen again. It has taken years to build my self-confidence, so I must find a balance. I must be tolerant and kind but never take any really bad shit. It is all good although I sometimes feel anxious and have lost a bit of weight. I am so happy most of the time, though I tend to become unnerved every now and again. I have no idea why. Pandora says my smile lights up my face and is like no other she has seen. Whilst alone, I am beginning to smile slightly less. Four weeks ago it was there all the time. Now my skin is feeling tight and my eyes are tired. I need my smile because without it, all I have is a face.

Our relationship is not conventional and relies heavily on words. It is more like a dream that is waiting to come true. Its beauty is the anticipation, I am sure of that. We are like love-struck teenagers, only without the intimacy. Inside our minds we are still very young and at our beautiful prime. *Perhaps we are simply afraid to flaunt our imperfect naked bodies?* We are both still attractive although insecure and vain. Maybe we secretly wish to re-enact a scene from 'Last Tango in Paris.' (We are both dramatic enough) although something is stopping us. The innocence is so appealing. Things often get sullied after the sex thing anyway.

Jude says, "Our relationship is better than that – it's spiritual, strong and above sex... We're too good to ruin it with all that gubbins."

It is a lovely sentiment although I want and endlessly fantasise about him. However, I worry that the real thing would be a letdown.

Yesterday, I went to his house again and he asked me, "Do you think we will ever have sex, Cathy? It's been so long for me; I've forgotten how to do it."

I blushed as I looked into his dark, beautiful but slightly cold eyes. "Of course we will one day – I'm sure."

I wonder if he says these things because he imagines I expect it. Perhaps he is just as frightened as me.

Pandora

Each time Eloise regaled Jude's stories and poetry, she looked different. She had such fire in her eyes and I was afraid for her. She had never looked that way before. I feared Jude's words were empty and perhaps a grooming technique – a game that could eventually destroy Eloise's world. She appeared to be letting go of reality. *Did he have a fervid scheme and would she ever be able to see it?*

***

April 31st - Eloise

It has only been a month since we found each other again, but things have moved at such a fast pace. Several lunches and non-stop messaging makes Pandora think it is too full-on after such a short space of time. She thinks that Jude has an evil plan to possess me entirely. Who cares if he does? She is such a worry-wart.

Chapter 2
Jude – By Pandora

It was May, 1986, when Eloise and I met Jude for the first time. Eloise was being her usual dramatic self, as she pined over her latest lost love, whilst guzzling beer and then laughing inanely – desperately trying to put him out of her mind.

Joe had been a sensible boy and Eloise seemed happy for a time. She tried so hard to curb her behaviour and impress him. After a while, he began to treat her like crap and all I could do was to watch her crumble, especially when he ended their relationship after two years. She was deeply depressed and found her grief impossible to come to terms with … until she met Jude.

We were in Spud-U-Like, a tacky eatery in Hampton, not far from our local pub. Two boys walked in and sat at the table beside us. They smiled and Eloise immediately homed in on the prettier of the two.

"Hello, gorgeous ladies. I'm Jude and this is Jake."

Jude lapped up the attention as Eloise chatted with him, gazing into his beautiful peepers all the while – and I was left with the booby-prize.

Jake just cordially nodded, probably sensing that I had no interest in him whatsoever. We made polite small talk whilst the other two were practically eating each other's heads.

Later we went back to Jude's small loft apartment, where he led Eloise to his bedroom. I tried to remain affable and jovial with Jake, and it was hard not to laugh because of the megalophonic din coming from Jude's bedroom.

Jude was a drifter and had no job. He claimed to be a decorator, although judging from the state of his flat it was doubtful. Soon Eloise and Jude became almost inseparable and she phoned me every day without fail to fill me in on all the gory details.

Each evening, as soon as she had finished work, she would go to him. Even then, he fancied himself as a bit of a poet and knew exactly how to capture a girl's heart. He was quite manipulative with his technique but it made her happy for a time.

Extracts from Eloise's journals

May 11th 1986

On Monday I decided to surprise Jude and cook him a nice meal. All we seem to do is go out and get drunk, so most of it is usually forgotten the next day. It will be nice to do something romantic for a change. He is having a tough time getting work at the moment and I worry about him not eating properly. I turned up at his flat with a bag of goodies and the intention of having a dreamy night. Jude answered the door, looking a bit worse for wear.

"Have you been drinking?" I asked, not all that bothered.

"No, I've just dropped some acid," he said, as I walked passed him into the hall.

This made me uncomfortable because even as a bit of a piss-head, I hate hard drugs.

"Oh, well I hope you're hungry," I said, as I unpacked the groceries.

"Why are you buying me fucking food? I've got my own fucking food!"

"It's a treat, what's wrong with that?"

"I'm not a fucking charity case."

"I didn't say you were. I just wanted to make you some dinner."

By now my eyes were blurred and it was hard not to cry.

"Don't cry, you pathetic little tart," he shouted, as he grabbed me by the throat.

He pinned me to the wall and stared with a look of hate, as I stood motionless.

It happened so quickly and felt like a dream, so took a few moments to sink in. Then it struck me that Jude's twisted face might be the last thing I would ever see. I tried to remain calm because my tears and fear were clearly making his temper worse. It was like a desperate attempt to survive and eventually he let go of my neck. My sight was blurred and my throat hurt as I pulled the door open and ran to the bus station. My body and soul ached as I headed home in disbelief, shock and with a heavy heart. As soon as I reached my house I rang Pandora and told her what had happened. She insisted I go to the police but I refused. However, I promised never to see Jude again.

May 12th 1986

This morning, I had resigned myself to the affair being over. Then mid-morning, the telephone rang.

"Can I come round, Eloise? We need to talk."

"I don't think it's a very good idea, Jude. I've got nothing to say to you."

"I'll understand if you don't want to see me again. I just want to explain and tell you how sorry I am, Babe."

"Okay, I'll let you have your say. I'm so confused and hurt and need to know why you acted that way."

"Okay, I'll be at yours in half an hour."

Jude arrived soon after, visibly shaken and full of remorse. My mother was in the garden so at least it felt safe.

Mum and Dad fight constantly and I am usually caught in the thick of it. Sometimes they hit me hard, especially if I interfere or sometimes just because they're drunk. I feel like their whipping boy at times, although Jude's behaviour has been much worse.

Mum bustled in and out with tea, unaware of what had happened. Jude explained that he was abandoned at birth and left in care. His birth name was Connor and was changed to Jude when he was adopted at the age of four. His new family already had children a lot older than him and were an extremely religious, strict unit. He was a naughty little ragamuffin and he alleged they disliked him from the start.   He was regularly beaten, shouted at and always left out of anything fun. Because of his dark looks the other kids would call him a gypsy or Paki.

He slept in a box room resembling a cell and was soon packed off to boarding school. He claimed that he could never develop normal relationships and his behavioural problems had worsened over the years. As soon as he was old enough, he left home and rarely saw his adoptive family. He said he felt so alone and often suffered racial abuse. The last straw for him had been a broken heart. The love of his life had left him, not long before we met, and he is still hurting about that. She refused to have sex until they were married and Jude was nowhere near ready for that commitment.

His story makes me feel so sorry for him although he does that very well himself. I have agreed to give him another chance although a foreboding still remains. The thought of being second best to the 'love of his life' is an added disappointment. I have an awful feeling that this relationship will prove to be hard work but I need to take that chance. Pandora thinks I am a sucker for a sob-story and a beautiful face. I am sure we can work our problems out together because we are similar in character. I still do mad things, especially when I drink although my moods are nowhere near as weird as his.

Pandora

After Jude had opened his heart, the constant spew of self-pity was never-ending. Sometimes they would meet in our local and I would have to suffer his ramblings also. He would smoke dope and sit for hours, looking morose and talking about himself. Every time they met he would go on and on, until Eloise saw her own childhood problems as miniscule in comparison, so felt guilty about feeling anything. She looked to Jude as some sort of tragic hero that could only be loved and admired. I would just listen in disbelief to his whining and roll my eyes. I would often receive a hard kick under the table from Eloise. Now she would forgive him anything. His regular outbursts and tantrums were always excused and he knew that – so did exactly as he pleased. Her tenacity was such that she forever inflicted pain upon herself and this was not the first time. She should have walked away and given herself some dignity. She was young however and thought that she loved him.

Jude began to go out on his own more so Eloise would do the same, albeit begrudgingly. She awoke one morning with the most dreadful stomach cramps and rushed to the bathroom. She found blood and other unspeakable gunk in her underwear. She rang me in a panic and I offered to accompany her to her GP. The doctor took some swabs and told her that she had contracted an STD. Eloise was mortified and went to see Jude that afternoon. I knew she would succumb to him however – accepting his spew of manipulative crap.

June 21st 1986 – Eloise

Shock is hardly the word to describe the way I feel at the moment. What a horrible day! I have been to see Jude and he has managed to talk his way back into my heart – not that he ever really left. I feel so dirty though...

"What have you done to me? I've got a fucking dose!" I shouted.

"I'm sorry, Eloise, I've had some problems down below too."

"But we've been together for months and I don't sleep around. I didn't give it to you, so who did?"

"I'm sorry; it was a couple of weeks ago when I was out with Jake. I was stoned and didn't know what I was doing. Some old slag handed it to me on a plate ... what's a boy to do?"

My stomach churned as I sensed that he had no remorse. He just expected forgiveness without question.

Then he added, "I caught up with Sharon last week and we had a little talk. I hope I haven't given it to her too."

"What, you slept with her?"

"Yes, she wanted me back, so gave in and let me have her cherry. It was really awkward and we both agreed it was a mistake straight afterwards, so you don't have to worry."

"Who the hell do you think you are, fucking Lord Byron?"

He laughed and seemed almost proud of the comparison. I sat on his sofa and cried for over an hour and not once did he so much as offer a cup of tea. Instead, he strummed badly on his guitar, trying to look wistful and smiling at me occasionally. *What was I to do*? I loved him so much and the thought of never seeing him again was more painful than what he had done.

"I'm going home, I need to think about what I'm gonna do. You've hurt me so badly, Jude."

"Fair enough. I'll catch up with you later."

As I walked to the door, Jude surprised me by suddenly switching to Emily Bronte mode. He jumped in front of me, looked deeply into my eyes and began with his seductive words.

"Don't leave me my, Cathy; the Heights will never be the same without you."

At that moment, I was reduced to a quivering wreck. *How the hell did he know that was my favourite book... film... song?*

"I'll always come back. You know that don't you, Heathcliff?" It just sort of fell out of my mouth.

Pandora

It was so touching; you would never have known they were both riddled with the clap and I was getting pretty tired of their badly-scripted soap-opera.

Soon all was forgiven and a course of antibiotics had saved the day. Their peculiar dalliance continued for a few more weeks. Eloise was either up in the clouds or down in the shit-pit – never anything in between, until the afternoon she received that phone call.

August 28th 1986 – Eloise

My world has become a dark place once again. Jude rang this morning.

"Hi, it's me," he sang. "Listen, I hate to tell you this, but Sharon's been in touch and we've decided to give it another go. She's coming over next week. I'm really sorry. We had some fun though, didn't we? Take care... Bye."

I am going to bed. Life is not something that I want to face today, or tomorrow for that matter.

Pandora

Jude made me so angry that I paid him a visit. I wanted to kill him. What went on that night has always remained between me and Jude; provided he can even remember. He was always so drugged up and could possibly have forgotten. Eloise would have never forgiven me if she knew.

If ever I tried to help she would call it interference and snap, "Pandora, You're not my fucking mother."

It took days for me to talk Eloise out of her bed although soon she was back to her normal self, and after a couple of months she seemed to forget all about Jude. We saw him at our local haunts a handful of times and he would call her over, but she just ignored him. After that he just seemed to disappear out of her life for what we thought would be forever.

Chapter 3
Books

Extracts from Eloise's journals
May 3rd 2012

Jude emailed one of his books to me yesterday, as a way of explaining what had happened to him during our many years apart.

I have read the whole thing in one sitting and have fallen more deeply in love with him at every turn of the page. He is so clever with his words which can whisk me away into a dream-like state for hours. He speaks of the cruelty he endured as a child and it makes for harrowing reading. I am happy to discover that the 'love of his life' had left him after five years with a broken heart – well happy for me anyway. He carried on with his wild ways, drug taking and numerous one night stands. He had looked for his birth mother and never managed to find her. He worked as a doorman and driver, involving himself with many a dubious character which allowed him to buy a house with dirty-money. Then in his late thirties, he had a terrible accident and injured his pelvis, rendering him partially disabled and wracked with constant pain. That part surprises me because he seems to walk without any obvious impediment – perhaps he has got used to it. He retired soon after and decided to abandon the drugs and live a quiet life alone with his pets. In solitude, hidden away from the cruel world, he began to write. He penned two biographies and three children's stories.

Jude has kept fairly quiet about his life post-1986, before sending me this, though he forever cryptically whinges about his sad life which is a bit annoying sometimes. At least after reading, I know more about what happened and why he acts the way he does. I am so impressed with the book, in spite of a few typos, that I want to see him. I need to hold him, love him and take the pain away.

I am driving to his house this afternoon because I feel the urge to see him. Never before have I turned up without prior arrangement. Our lunch dates are usually at the same time, same place and then back to his house for an hour. It is always regimented and quite ludicrous – although it does make me smile. I worry that he will be cross or, worse; I will find him up to no good. My spontaneity has taken over however, so I am going anyway. It is not in my nature to pussy-foot and dance to anyone's tune but with Jude it is different. I must overlook his mood swings because he is a sensitive soul with astonishing talents. I realise the folly and danger of hero-worship, but he is worthy of my out-of-character reserve. However, today I am taking a chance and hope it will pay off.

May 4th

Well I went. As my car pulled into his drive, he saw me from the lounge window and rushed to greet me at the door. He looked so happy to see me and we hugged for many minutes. Our hugs are always long and intense, as though we are one and can never let go. I felt a stirring that was hard to control but managed to hold back. The urge to kiss him passionately was strong although I thought tongues were reserved for young people and he might find my advances ridiculous. He seemed even taller than usual which made me feel like a dainty little princess, held by her strong knight. It surprised me when he began to sob as he kissed the top of my head. His tears fell into my hair which, as usual, was unkempt in its natural wavy state and now all soggy on top. *'Why was he crying*?' I wondered. I had never seen him weep before. We managed to contain ourselves and the waterworks subsided just as quickly as they had begun. I wiped his tears and lifted my finger to my mouth, trying to be poetic, as I knew this would impress him.

"If I swallow your tears, it means that you're mine forever," I said, without feeling the least bit cringey.

A broad and radiant smile appeared upon his tearstained face.

"Why were you crying, Jude?"

"Because you came to me as if you knew it was what I wanted."

"Was it what you wanted?"

"Oh yes. I was feeling very low and you must have sensed it – you are my angel of mercy."

Jude pulled away and went to make some tea as I sat in the lounge with a still racing heart.

"Did you finish my book then?" he shouted from the kitchen as he busied himself.

"Yes, I did. By the way, did your hips get better in the end?"

"Oh no, I am in agony every day, but I try to overcome it. It's a battle and some days are worse than others."

As he returned to the lounge with tea and toast, I noticed he had suddenly developed a limp. There is no reason for me to disbelieve he suffers pain but perhaps he was exaggerating a bit after my comments. He does seem to enjoy wallowing in gloom from time to time. I doubt he is an out and out liar; maybe he is sometimes just a tad economical with the truth. No matter, I still love him warts and all. That is true love in my world – unconditional. He needs someone like me; perhaps other women have fled because of his foibles. He has been to hell and back so I excuse his little faults – I even find them quite endearing sometimes. He has come a long way and I have no wish to be over critical just because he has imperfections. I now realise that he craves attention – and who can blame him? He has never had much of that to be fair. I have many faults and have learned to embrace them so, of course, I must offer the same courtesy to Jude. Mum and Dad were always distant and called me names like 'thick' and 'drama-queen' – they had little time for me. My childhood was full of self-doubt and questions although clearly not as bad as Jude's. Self-worth is the key to life and I want to help Jude build his esteem. I simply refuse to assassinate his character, he deserves better. I have learned not to be critical of myself so have no business judging him.

We snuggled on the sofa for an hour or so and I wanted to stay there forever. I told him that this would be the perfect way to die – together in each other's arms. He laughed and held me even tighter, until I could hardly breathe. It was uncomfortable but felt so good. His heart was beating in perfect rhythm as I lay my head on his chest. The gentle sound made me drift into a glorious to sleep. Suddenly, Jude sprang from the sofa and stood bolt-upright. My heart almost leapt from my chest.

"WALKIES TIME!"

Not wishing to interfere with his routine, I sat up, rubbing my eyes and said, "Okay, I'll get going."

"Do you fancy coming with us?"

"That would be lovely, thank you," I answered with a ridiculous grin.

"We can go to the lake and see the horses; I'll go and get some fruit."

We had a magical afternoon, walking, laughing, eating, holding hands and taking pictures. Jude has invited me into his private sanctuary of a world and I am triumphant.

May 16th

My first novel, which had taken years to write, is complete and Jude has offered to give it an edit. His grammar is not the best but I have decided to indulge him anyhow. I have emailed it with some trepidation. I worry it may anger him, as he knows much of my story is based on personal experience. Perhaps he will disapprove of the heroin's raucous behaviour, think I am a tart or learn things about me that should be dead and buried. There are references to her many sexual encounters and I wonder if this will make him jealous. He does seem to have gone a bit quiet today. Perhaps he is busy with my book. Oh well, hopefully he will contact me later...

May 20th

I was right. He is having a mammoth sulk and ignoring me. I have heard nothing for days; he seems to have ceased all contact. I am beside myself. He has been angry with me before but never for this length of time and I am checking my messages like mad – but nothing. There is no way I am going to contact him first, I still have my pride... It has become a bit of a waiting game.

May 24th

It has been just over a week since we last made contact and today Jude emailed. He has sent me my edited novel and a kiss. I replied and asked him what was wrong. He told me that everything was fine although he disliked my book. This is really strange and a step too far. He just dislikes the content plain and simple but refuses to admit it. He said it is so badly written it would make any publisher laugh. He can be rude and spiteful sometimes, hardly better than my bullying ex-husband. Actually no! He could never be that bad and has a beautiful soul. He does have a peculiar mind-set however, and I think it's about time to tell him what I actually think about his carry-on. Hopefully he will change his tune and have a bit more empathy for me.

May 25th

Bloody hell, he is cross with me now. We have fallen out big-time because I dared to question his motive for saying my book was shit. He called me a spoiled brat who could not write for toffees. So I called him a nut-job and told him to fuck off and boil his self-serving, fat head. He replied and said that I am an angry and deranged person who has hurt him badly, so all contact will cease. How the hell did I hurt him? I only retaliated to his rudeness and now I am the bad guy. I cannot fathom him sometimes.

***

I have just returned from Pandora's house. She opened the door and found me sobbing. My intention was to appear cool but her look of concern broke me down. My phone was by my side for the whole evening as I willed a message from Jude. We watched a DVD of Wuthering Heights which Pandora hates.

"Why did you bring it, Eloise?" You're just torturing yourself even more.

"I just need to watch it. I feel closer to Jude."

"There was no need to watch her reaction. She would be rolling her eyes in despair. If only she would be there for me and stop judging my decisions.

"Sometimes you behave as unhinged as him," she said laughing – It was clear that she meant it.

Every so often, I looked at my phone for messages. Pandora stared at the TV, pretending not to notice. The look on my face told her there were none. She tried to convince me that he would be in touch and was simply playing games. She was attempting to pacify and humour me – it was obvious. She says that he toys with my mind and I imagine she hopes we are over. None of this sits right in her mind. She fails to understand.

May 30th

Jude messaged me this morning as though nothing had happened and things feel normal again. *Why would he play me like Pandora suggests*? It makes no sense at all. He just has funny moods. We have spoken a lot today and he has been nothing but kind and sweet. We are having lunch tomorrow and he says he is giving me a key to his house. He wants me to come and go as I please and treat it as my own. He wants to leave it to me in his will because I am all that he has. His gesture has shocked me. Mind you, the thought of him dying is something I refuse to even think about. I must go and tell Pandora that she is wrong about him.

"He must love me to offer me his house, Pandora," I shrieked.

"That's lovely. I hope it's not just words and he means to treat you right."

"He does. He says he'll sell the house one day and buy us a place in France. Can you imagine?"

"Sounds idyllic." She answered, sounding hardly enthused.

"He even suggested we start a business – a doggy day centre. I only have to close my eyes to picture the scene. He speaks as he writes, holding me captive with beautiful visions. I swear he can talk in colour."

"It's a gift, and one he can use to his advantage. He knows exactly what he's doing."

"What do you mean? We all do it! We all manipulate people to an extent. Sometimes it's a good thing, saying nice things to make people happy."

"I suppose, but why do you let him get to you so much? Why don't you either accept his mood swings or just get rid?"

"Oh I could never let him go. He's the love of my life. We rarely have words face-to-face. It's that bloody internet, it misconstrues everything."

"Well good luck with it. Perhaps I'm just a bit cynical."

Pandora

It was those wonderful romantic moments that pulled Eloise in and she had no intention of losing them. She was letting him get the better of her. She had taken a positive grasp on her life before meeting Jude. I feared she was slowly being controlled again because of her dangerously trusting nature.

Chapter 4
Internet Creep

June 9th

I am gobsmacked, what the hell is going on? My cousin sent me a couple of jokes this morning via email and I read them first. I wanted to read Jude's message last so I could savour it. I was horrified to find a picture of his erect penis and wondered why on earth he had done such a thing. Our relationship is still pretty much sexless which makes this all the more bizarre. Pandora thinks perhaps it was meant for somebody else.

Jude is on my ignore list for the rest of today. He has obviously flipped. Pictures of knobs are not in the least bit funny. He has treated me with disrespect and it is just plain weird; especially after all the crap he spouts about the purity of our relationship. He often reminds me of how perfect Cathy and Heathcliff were and how they never had sex... what bollocks! Maybe he posted it to me by mistake. Perhaps he relieves himself by cyber-whoring. Yuk!! I feel sick at the thought.

June 10th

Jude is bugging me with emails, asking what is wrong. I am going to challenge him this time, it is too much. He has just replied and says it was just a joke and I should lighten up. I messaged him back.

'I am disgusted. What on earth were you thinking?' I asked him.

'Oh grow up. It's not like you've never seen a dick before is it?'

'I am grown up; I think it's you who are acting like a hormonal schoolboy. It's so out of character for you and in terribly bad taste – have you gone mad?'

'You're just a prude.'

'No I'm not. You're a weirdo.'

'I just wanted you to see what you have to look forward to.'

'This is too much; I think your mask is slipping. Fuck right off!'

***

"Pandora, whatever will I do?"

"I don't think he is quite right in the head, Eloise. He lives with such a rigid routine and likes to test you all the time. I hate it when you get upset and all in all he doesn't really make you happy, does he?"

I gave her one of my looks and quickly changed the subject.

She could tell I was miserable. I have lost at least fourteen pounds in weight and my smile is often absent. Jude and I have been estranged for three days and my heart is breaking.

June 14th

There are so many doubts running through my mind right now. I need to find out if he is talking to women online. I am quite the internet detective when I want to be. I think I know just the way to catch him out.

Trying to hack into his computer has proved futile; he must be smarter than I thought. My attempts to read his emails have failed. Every password I tried was wrong. The names of his dogs, his birth name, his birth-mother's name, his first teddy bear, his street name, his birth date, and even combinations of words and dates – nothing works. A fake profile on Facebook should do the trick.

***

Now I am a girl called Susie. To avoid suspicion my mystery woman also writes books and would naturally try to befriend other authors. I have added friends so it looks like the real deal and a random photograph from the internet. Susie is a beautiful blonde in her mid to late twenties, who enjoys books and photography – right up his street! As Susie, I have friend requested Jude.

This is so scary. Perhaps I will discover something I would rather not. It is shameful. I have set a honey-trap for Jude. The need to be certain I can trust him has forced me to do this. If he is stringing other women along or even using them to alleviate his frustrations, I have no idea what will come of us.

***

Oh my God, it worked. I regret it now but simply needed to know. Jude has messaged Susie and really quickly too.

'Hello. So you write books do you, Susie?' Jude asked.

'Yes, children's fiction.'

'Oh, me too. Your profile says you're single. Why has a beautiful girl like you not got a boyfriend?'

It made me almost throw up and I wanted it to stop. I kept my cool however and answered.

'I recently broke up with my boyfriend and I want to be single for a while. Do you have a girlfriend?'

I bit my lip in anticipation and dreaded the answer although somehow I knew what it would be.

'No, free and single, me!'

My heart was breaking and I had to end the conversation.

'I have to go – nice talking to you.'

At that point, I logged off as my head fell toward my knees and I sobbed inconsolably – not that there was anyone there to take the pain away. Seconds later Charlie breezed into the lounge and asked what was wrong.

"I've just watched a really sad film," I blubbed, trying to pull myself together.

If my chauvinistic son, horribly influenced by his father, had known what was really going on, he would have undoubtedly gloated.

Charlie just laughed and breezed out again like teenagers do. He rarely says two words to me anyway.

Jude has fallen for my game and it has been as easy as pie. *How will he talk himself out of this one?* He will undoubtedly try – he is so good at that, but I have decided I am having none of it.

Today I have ignored all of Jude's phone calls and messages. He has just sent me an email begging for a reply. He says that he has misses me and is worried. It is very late and way past his usual strict bedtime routine. I notice he has left messages in Susie's private inbox as well. I dread reading them but will have to look.

***

'Where are you Susie?' he asked the non-existent tart.

This is ludicrous. I am jealous of someone that does not exist.

He pressed on with stoic insistence. 'Is this a wind-up?'

'Why won't you answer me?'

Now I am angry. So angry, that the feelings of hurt have almost vanished.

I am going to confront him and tell him exactly what I have done.

***

Well, we have had it out and he has managed to turn the whole thing round onto me of course.

'How devious! I knew it was you!' he insisted.

'Did you fuck! You're are a bleeding liar and internet pest.'

'I knew it was you. I was just playing along.'

'Liar.'

'Fucking mad bitch!'

'I have been so stupid.'

'You've had an unhappy past and it's made you bitter, Eloise,' he said in his insufferable, patronising manner.

'Stop projecting your own shit onto me. You are the mad one – quit putting me down.'

'You must be hurting so badly inside from your past. It's made you vile and angry.'

'What the fuck are you on about? Look, I've had enough; you are a fucking loony with all your me-me-me-attitude. Nothing you say makes any sense. Please leave me alone. I don't want to hear from you again.'

I think that, at last, I have grown some balls. He is fucking with my mind. Perhaps not deliberately, but at this moment I hate him and am actually relieved it is all over. Yes I am angry and have every right to be; he has driven me to it. I am surprised at how patient I have been with him up until this point to be honest.

June 21st

Now there is a different kind of stress to greet me every morning. The routine niceties, which I was wearing of anyway, have been replaced by relentless stalking and begging. It has only been a week since our fall-out. I am feeling strong however and know that Jude is wrong for me.

***

Like a fool, I had given Jude my address when we were sending each other presents. He once even sent me some expensive dog food for my pooches which I thought was very sweet at the time.

***

Now, every day I am bombarded with flowers, letters and soft toys. I swear he is trying to land me in trouble with my son and ex-husband. They would be sure to give me grief if they found out – and he knows that.

June 24th

For the past ten days I have tried to ignore Jude. Now he is sending me novellas and poems, highlighting the good times and innocent purity of our passion. They are truly beautiful apart from the mistakes. I must not slip. I always read them however – how could I not?

June 27th

Jude is so sorry and desperate to meet with me again. We have spoken on the phone a couple of times and he has been nothing but nice. Even when I insult him, he just takes it on the chin. I have been getting away with murder and he fully accepts my disgust at his picture. He says he will never do such a thing again. Gradually, he is knocking down the wall I have built around myself.

June 29th

Jude has reclaimed my heart and soul. He swears he knew I was Susie all along. He is clearly asexual, so his pursuing others makes no sense anyway. I really want to believe him and hope I am not making a huge mistake. Now all I have to do is convince Pandora. I know she will be disappointed. She will think I am gullible and climb onto her soapbox again. She is never unkind about Jude exactly. She just keeps telling me to be careful and thinks he is mental. She worries about me far too much.

Chapter 5
Birthdays

July 11th

My novel is coming along really slowly. I have made so many changes; I must have rewritten it at least fifteen times. My aged laptop is not ideal and I can ill afford a new one. My forty-fourth birthday is tomorrow and Jude says he has something special in mind.

My son, Charlie has planned to take me for a birthday meal and Jude is not happy. I suggested that we meet today, spend the afternoon together and perhaps have a meal later. We will be together for the best part of today which I am really looking forward to. Jude is peeved that I must spend my actual birthday with my son, although I could hardly refuse. I am going to meet Jude later and we will walk the dogs. I am not sure what will happen between the walk and the meal later. The anticipation is what keeps our love alive.

***

I drove to Jude's place just after lunch and he greeted me with a long, lingering hug.

"I've got a hard-on now, Cathy."

His off-the-wall, cheekier than usual, retort took me by surprise but, as always, I simply put it down to his being random, eccentric and mysterious. He is beginning to throw innuendo into conversation a lot more now and if I pull a face, he just laughs and says he is joking. It drives me mad. I hate it when people do that although Jude gets away with things I would never usually tolerate. I felt very liberated for some strange reason however and instead of my usual faux coyness, I went hell for leather and gave him a knowing look, before kissing him full on the mouth. All the innocence and lack of gay abandon was getting on my tits – I wanted his cock inside me. It was the first time I had actually felt this desperate urge and it surprised me as much as it did him. He knew exactly what I wanted because, without speaking, I begged with my eyes to be taken to his room. We sort of glided to our destination, still attached by our hungry lips and fell onto his bed. He lay on top of me and then pulled himself upward, his deep dark eyes gazing into the sea-blue mirrors of my insatiable soul. I moved up toward him, put my mouth to his with a gentle lick and then softly bit his bottom lip. He put his tongue inside my mouth for the first time, but only a little. We remained that way for what seemed like forever, our lips touching with the subtlety of butterfly wings. I wanted him to undress me and fuck me with aggression. I felt ashamed but needed him like nothing else. Even if he had herpes, was clinically insane or the devil incarnate – I wanted him with a passion unknown to me. Again, we instinctively pulled away. *Why do we torture ourselves so?*

"Right, let's go and get your birthday present, "he said, as if none of the past few moments had happened. The disappointment was etched on my face; I could feel the muscles tighten and tried hard to look jolly.

"Where is it then?"

"Round the corner in a shop, come on..."

"Ooh, how exciting!" I said, trying to look enthusiastic.

It was a lovely gesture although I would have preferred sex. I suppose we are not ready yet. We walked hand in hand to the local shops where Jude led me into an electrical store.

"Afternoon, I've come to collect the PC that I've purchased for my wife."

"You shouldn't have spent so much on me Jude."

"You are worth every penny, my Cathy and you need it to write."

I had never loved him more at that moment and adored the way he had called me 'his wife.'

He took the computer from the counter and we walked out of the shop.

"You called me your wife!"

"Well you will be," he answered, smiling his beautiful smile.

"This is the happiest day of my life, Jude. Thank you."

*** *

We went for our Indian meal and, as usual, attracted attention with our loud voices. Jude joked with the waiter, telling him we were slightly deaf which is true, but funny nonetheless. He said he should have worn a turban to blend in – joking about his skin colour as always. I think his laughter is a sham to be honest, and not knowing his roots bothers him greatly. We were like children, all the while giggling and holding hands. After the meal, we walked back to Jude's house arm-in-arm. I love how tall he is and feel safe beside him. We watched some TV as we lay together on the sofa. Soon it was time for me to go. I wanted to stay with him all night so badly but thought I had better go home. I worried that I may take leave of my senses and do something outrageously naughty again. Perhaps there are still trust issues and fears of being hurt. Whatever it is – we are a most peculiar pair.

July 12th 2012

Charlie and I had a lovely meal and that was it really. Happy birthday to me! I missed Jude terribly all day.

July 15th

My book has become a bit of a chore to be honest. Editing wearies the soul and I have neither the patience nor wherewithal to give it credence nowadays. I am either obsessed and work like a Trojan, or just cannot face writing for days on end. Sometimes I lose track of time and forget to check my emails and Jude gets the huff. Everything seems to be about him and his feelings. He is very good at the old sweet-talk although he appears to have no empathy for anyone but himself. He has sent me a list of suggestions and edits for my story because he has only proof-read the grammar part of it so far (oh the irony!) He phoned me to ask what I thought about his ideas and my mood was a little grim.

"But it's my story and I like it the way it is," I protested politely.

"I know, but I am trying to help you improve it, that's why I bought you the computer."

"Yes, but you want me to completely change it, you may as well just write it yourself."

"You are so fucking ungrateful, why are you so cruel to me, especially after I bought you such an expensive gift?"

"I've never asked you for anything and gifts are supposed to be just that, not a bargaining tool."

"I bought you the computer because I care and to spur you on with your book."

"So let me get this straight. You've bought me a computer so you can control what I write, and if it doesn't agree with your double-standard morality, I have to change stuff?"

"You are so angry. It must be the sadness in your life that's made you so vile and angry."

"Why do you keep bloody saying that? It's nonsense."

"You're hurting me, Cathy; I've had so much hurt in my life from my parents, girlfriends and friends, I can't take anymore."

"Well I'm just starting to realise why you *are* alone, it's because you are impossible to reason with. The only person you love is you, you fucking nut job."

"You're aggressive, Eloise." (He still drops the 'Cathy' when he is annoyed with me.)

"I am not! Listen, I've had enough. Please don't contact me again."

"But I bought you a computer which was very generous of me."

"Oh, stick it up your fucking arse, Heathcliff!"

I have come to the end of my tether with him. I will ask Pandora to drive me to his house and dump the fucking computer at his door so I can make a quick getaway. Actually, sod it! He has given me so much grief; I am going to keep the bloody thing.

July 18th

Jude continues to bombard me with his poetry and stories. I am holding my own and refuse to acknowledge them however. I think I am over him because I have really seen his true colours now. Sometimes, I am sad and tearful, especially if something triggers a memory of him, like a song or TV show, of which there are many.

The good times were really something else, but it is too hard walking that tight-rope because I never know which side I am going to fall off. It is time to concentrate on work and he is holding me back. He wants to be the best writer and it seems to be turning into a competition.

July 28th

Tomorrow is Jude's birthday. He still pesters me, refusing to let me go. I cannot go back to him. He has been quiet over the past couple of days however, and in a sick way I miss his weirdness. It is a relief to have my life back although I feel bad because tomorrow is his birthday. The thought of him being alone haunts me even though he has been alone for many years anyway. This year I had promised him it would be different and special. I am consumed with guilt, so must get him a little something at least and post it.

***

Money is tight, so I have found Jude a nice blue polo shirt in a sale and bought him a card too. The colour will look gorgeous on him. I am going to send it now.

***

I feel better for getting Jude a present although I walked back from town with a heavy heart. It is such a beautiful day and I want to be with him. Now I am crying – silly cow!

***

This evening I have relented. I made Jude a video to the tune of, 'Don't give up on us,' by Jason Mraz, using photographs from our time together. I hesitated for a long while before sending it, and then finally pushed the button around 11.30 pm when I knew he would be online. Within minutes, I received a message.

"Thank you, my Cathy. That's made my day."

Now, I will probably cry myself to sleep.

***

Pandora

Eloise was being sucked into Jude's surreal game again. Soon they would be together – until the next drama of course.

Chapter 6
No Sex, Drugs or Rock n Roll

August 1st

Jude and I plan to spend more time together during August. I love it when summer is on its cusp and I will have more free time. We are having fewer spats (mostly due to restraint and patience.) My restraint is probably a little steadier although Jude is trying really hard to balance his mood.

August 2nd

Charlie is due to go on holiday with his father this Friday for a couple of weeks. Hopefully I will be able to spend some evenings with Jude for a change. Perhaps I could even stay over for a couple of nights. At least I will have more flexibility, without the need to explain where I am all the time. Earlier I was talking to Jude on Facebook and we were planning the month ahead. Unfortunately, he has gone into another sulk because I cut short our chat when I needed to pop out for a minute.

'Just driving Charlie to the gym – be right back.'

At first it never occurred to me that he would mind at all. However, upon my return, I found a morose Jude, writing the oddest things and complaining that he felt unloved.

'The brat is seventeen. Why do you have to drive him everywhere?'

'It's raining really heavily and I don't mind giving him lifts and don't call him a brat!'

He disappeared offline after that and has not been in touch since. I am crying again – I fucking hate crying and have wept rather a lot during the past few months. I should try and get some sleep. He will be in touch tomorrow.

August 3rd

This morning, Jude sent me his normal early message and kisses as if nothing had happened. He told me he had gone to bed early with a headache. I have no desire to argue; at least he is in a better mood now, so I can look forward to seeing him later. He gets away with murder, he really does, although I am learning how to pacify him and my effort is worthwhile. His good side is so adorable. I love the way he snorts when he laughs.

* * *

The drive to Jude's house was exhilarating. The excitement of seeing him again is always my favourite part. I get the strangest feelings of anticipation and euphoria as I listen to Magic radio full blast, and sing along to all the romantic oldies. When I arrived, Jude looked furtive and even a little sad. There was no strangulating hug or kiss – nothing! Something was wrong and it made me feel anxious – it was like waiting outside a teacher's office, about to be scolded. As soon as we sat down in the lounge, he told me that in a few days it would be the anniversary of his sister's death. He sobbed as he spoke of his loss and I held him tightly, until my shoulder was sodden with his tears. I found his emotional outburst confusing however, because he had always spoken of his family with nothing but malice.

"So your sister was nicer than the rest of your family then?"

"Oh yes," he replied, his face still damp, looking agitated by my question. "She was the only one who cared."

I had no reason to disbelieve him, though thought it odd that he had never mentioned this wonderful sister before.

"I visit his grave every year alone; it's always such a difficult time."

"Do you want me to come with you then?"

"No, it's okay, I don't want to bother you with all that."

"Well the offer's there."

Jude was quiet for most of my visit and we parted company cordially, but it was awkward and completely devoid of romantic nuance – massive letdown!

August 4th

Jude's martyrdom has irked me a bit. The closer I get to him, the more I despair at his strange behaviour. I tend to keep quiet and just listen to his ramblings for the most part. It is much easier than the hell I would find myself in without him. His histrionic carry-on is now causing me uncertainty. At first, I found it endearing because my belief is that real men cry. But now my instincts make me question his sincerity. Sometimes he is strong and well-adjusted and his only sentiment is love. Other times he is an emotional wreck who can turn on the waterworks in the blink of an eye, especially if he is cross with me. That could be it! Perhaps these stories of his tragedy are fantasy. Maybe he is just annoyed with me and refuses to admit it, so comes up with ridiculous tales to seek my attention. *Can he mimic despair and tears?* If that is the case, then what an actor! I am probably just getting carried away with my thoughts. No one is perfect – I should be more patient with him – he has been through so much and this is unfeeling of me. At least now I know that if we argue he will always come back. This causes me to worry less as I become used to his pattern of behaviour – though I still hate fighting with him. I refuse to turn into a complete yes-woman however, and will save my assertiveness for his more monumental blunders.

August 9th

Charlie has gone away with his father now and I am free for a while. The past few days have been difficult and my online conversations with Jude are strained. I am very excited at the thought of us being together more but his mood is still peculiar.

Yesterday on the anniversary of his sister's death, Jude visited the grave. He took all day about it, so goodness knows what he did there. He probably took his bag of fruit and walked the dogs at the same time. I phoned him this morning to see if he was alright.

"How did it go?"

"How did you expect it to go? It was fucking awful!"

"I just wanted to make sure you were okay, Jude."

"No, I'm not, and what do you care anyway, I bet you had a lovely day?"

"I offered to come with you though, and you said you didn't want me to."

"Oh you didn't mean it … empty words, Eloise, you know what it meant to me and you didn't bother your arse to support me. You never ask how I feel, it's always about you."

'That's bloody rich,' I thought, but said nothing because he was clearly upset and talking gibberish.

"I'll speak to you tomorrow, sorry you're so upset. Goodnight," I said, hastily ending the call, before saying something I would later regret.

This time I know he will be fine in the morning – two weeks, or even a month. Whatever the time scale, he will be in touch; I can bet my life on it now. I have a feeling he will message me tomorrow – I hope so – why would he waste this precious time we have together? Anyhow, tonight I will sleep soundly and free of tears. I am learning…

August 10th

Jude's blowing hot and cold is a complete mystery to me. He appears to love me although it is the strangest love I have ever known. Pandora thinks he is deranged, though I would prefer to call him damaged. It does make me doubt the claims in his book of finding a good place in his mind. Everything he wrote in his self-help biography was nothing like the Jude I know. If he thinks his mind is now stable, he must be delusional. In fact, one could be forgiven if they doubted his actual story. He seems to thrive on pain and loves pity. *Is his sexual restraint just another game?* Perhaps he has prostate trouble, impotence or even some disease. Pandora sees him through her own eyes which are quite different to mine. She tells me off for putting things to the back of my mind. She sees it as a weakness, where I see it is strength.

Jude also claimed he was prescribed prescription drugs for pain, depression and psychosis shortly after his accident. Apparently he decided to bin his medicine and suffer the pain instead. His strength and bravery are noble and he hates drugs because he abused them in his youth. He was recently given a root canal without anaesthetic – or so he says. *Would a dentist agree to that?* There are so many questions and contradictions.

August 13th

Today, I visited Jude and he was pretty much back to his old self. It is such a shame we have wasted the last few days, but he has been out of sorts. We have never laughed so much and I am happier now. Jude played all of our favourite tunes on his Wurlitzer and then we closed our eyes and pressed the button, selecting something random. That was the funniest part. Jude just stood there; ready to move his dodgy hips like Elvis, only to hear Wuthering Heights by Kate Bush. He carried on dancing all the same and then attempted one of Kate's high kicks – it was hysterical. He looked like a demented fool – I thought it was cute and funny. Later he took one of his guitars off the wall and started to play – if you can call it playing! It was just a few random twangs with an ever-so-serious face. Jimi Hendrix he is not. I was embarrassed for him and told him he was great. He is a bit deluded about certain talents he claims to have but how could I tell him they are shit? The grammar edit on my book had left something to be desired when I studied it properly and I am hardly the expert myself. It was much worse than I had previously thought. I deleted his version without letting on of course. No wonder he has to pay so much for editors – I thought it sounded a bit steep. I think he should stick to taking photographs. I must admit, the more I get to know him, the more I secretly snigger and take the piss, especially when telling Pandora about him. He is a fabulous topic for discussion, with the amusing anecdotes and his cranky ways. His dark-side still troubles me a little but I can handle it.

August 15th

Today we had lunch and walked the dogs for six miles – I was knackered and wonder how he manages all that walking with his pain. We took a picnic and it was a cool beautiful day. We came to a field that was full of cows and a bull which began chasing us. Jude grabbed my hand and pulled me through the other side of the fence just in time.

"That was handy!"

"Who are you calling Gandhi, you cheeky bitch?"

Still making jokes about his skin colour … he made me laugh until I cried.

We sat by a stream and ate a picnic, watching the sun make little rainbows in the water. Jude took lots of pictures of me, as well as the wildlife – he is such a gifted photographer – I have to be honest and at least it makes up for the guitar-strumming and bad grammar. Then he picked a small piece of rosemary that was growing by the stream and put it into my mouth – it tasted like heaven. It never occurred to me that it might be covered in dog's pee or something worse. We arrived back at his house at teatime and flopped onto his couch. We held each other until we fell asleep and woke up an hour later feeling hungry.

After we had eaten, we watched television and were still glued at the hip. Every so often, I could feel Jude's hand slide down my back towards my bum. I thought it might be prudent to push it away but did no such thing. Instead, I let him rub my backside as I lay motionless. I was too afraid to appear excited (although I was.) I thought it might make me look like a tart, so remained motionless like a fucking buffoon. He was feeling my knickers – I could tell, trying to make out the shape and size. Thank God I had a nice sexy pair on! My legs were shaved and my lady-garden was pruned to perfection. I had cleaned anything that was unpleasant out of my belly-button and brushed my teeth until they hurt. Eventually I sat up and looked straight into his wonderful eyes. This was the red light to go. My subliminal pleas were answered and he kissed me with a passion that made me moist down below. His tongue filled my mouth so my own was unable to move. I almost choked but would have gladly suffocated at that moment. Suddenly his hands were everywhere – all over my boobs, my arse and my crotch.

Then he stopped quite abruptly and said, "I don't think we're quite ready. I don't want our relationship sullied."

What the fuck? I felt like a dirty stupid old fool. I have no idea what he was playing at and after his incessant chatter and tea drinking, as if nothing had happened, I decided to go. I told him that I needed to get back for my dogs. He insisted that I was welcome to stay, but my feeling of confusion and rejection made for my need to be alone. So here I am again – totally befuddled.

August 16th

A very odd message has appeared on my laptop this morning.

'Why did you rush off last night, Cathy?'

'Well, I felt a bit awkward after we … you know!'

'You, you, you… It's all about you. Not once did you ask how I felt!'

'You didn't ask how I felt either, Jude.'

'Well I wanted you to stay the night.'

'You could've fooled me.'

'I know I slowed things down, Cathy, but I wanted you to ask why.'

'You said we weren't ready, so I wasn't going to ask you to elaborate – what more is there to say on the subject?'

'But I wanted you to ask about my feelings, Cathy.'

'Well, I'm not a fucking clairvoyant.'

'I felt you really didn't want me. You were all stiff.'

'I did want you Jude; I was just a bit nervous.'

'I think we should have a break, Eloise.'

'Okay, contact me when you're ready.'

As soon as he called me Eloise I knew he was angry, although I still have no firm idea as to why. I am devastated and it is impossible to reason with him when he is like this. Is he testing me, playing games or just plain mad? I will let it lie for a bit.

August 24th

It has been over a week since I last spoke to Jude. Charlie has just returned from Portugal and this past week has been such a waste … just twiddling my thumbs on my own. I have been seeing more of Pandora these past weeks in between the arguments. We have even booked a holiday together in Italy this September. She has found a lovely villa in the sticks and talked me into going, I think she wants to get me away from Jude if I am honest. Perhaps this is the finish of us anyway and I will just have to get on with things. Pandora insists that we should go out more before the summer ends, perhaps to the local music pub – I think she feels sorry for me. Although my feelings of sadness are at their worst, I am much calmer inside which is something I suppose.

August 26th

Oh fuck! I have to go with Frank and Charlie to a University open day in an hour and we will be there all day. Jude messaged me this morning and said he is sorry. He explained that it has been so long since his last relationship, he needed time to get his head around this one. Now he wants to see me as soon as possible and I have to go out…

***

Unfortunately I was forced to lie and say I was meeting Pandora. He would flip if he knew I was spending the day with Charlie's father. He would never understand that these things just have to be done and spending time with Frank is actually a pain in the arse. I hate lying to him. Jude says not to worry; we can catch up another day (with a hint of disdain in his voice.) Still, he only has himself to blame.

***

Well, the University trip to Bangor went well and Charlie really wants to go there. I texted Jude several times during the course of the day, mostly, whilst sitting on the loo – charming! Jude has begged me to visit him tomorrow, so of course I will. Despite his regular hissy-fits, we seem to become even closer after each one.

August 27th

It was a lovely day today. Jude and I had lunch and then went back to his house for a bit of a cuddle. However, he seems far too preoccupied with what I have been up to in his absence.

"Did you see much of Pandora when we fell out?"

"No, not really."

"Good, she is a bad influence on you because she doesn't like me."

"Oh, I'm sure that's not true, Jude."

"She isn't your best friend, I am, aren't I, Cathy?"

"Yes, of course."

"I'm glad to hear it because you are my world."

I loved it when he said that. He rarely says that he loves me, just rather hints at it –although I know he does. I will never push myself on him again – he needs more time. If only I had said no to Pandora's holiday idea. Jude will hate me going away and still knows nothing about it. I wish I could tell Jude things without him flying off the handle. It feels wrong to keep things from him.
I lied about the university trip, amongst other things, and am frightened to mention the holiday. His strong feelings are wonderful although perhaps a tad too possessive. He even complains when I see my family or friends. I wish his crazy moods would disappear and never come back – then there would be no need to pussy-foot or hide away. He frightens me sometimes. Perhaps I am being overly sensitive. Summer is drawing to a close again. I like the autumn but dread winter. I find it really depressing although Jude can keep me warm.

Chapter 7
Holiday

September 2nd

My second book is coming along slowly and I sometimes struggle to find enthusiasm. I have been bombarding publishers and agents with my first effort and have only had one reply which was a 'no thanks.' Perhaps it is a waste of time but I need to make some money of my own. I am too easily distracted with one thing and another although, oddly, my own experience still inspires my stories, and seem to mirror my own life but I never use real names.

The thought of telling Jude about my holiday fills me with dread. I will have to tell him today. I shall take the coward's way out and do it by email – face to face is just too much. I will message him in an hour or so, once I have summoned the courage.

***

Okay, so now he knows and is not a happy bunny. He tried desperately to come across as cool, although I know he is really pissed off about it.

"When are you going?"

"September 15th."

"Why didn't you tell me before?"

"No reason, it just hasn't cropped up in conversation, it's only for a week."

"As long as you don't flirt around blokes."

"Don't be silly, you know I'm not like that."

"Well okay, I suppose there's nothing I can do about it. I hope you enjoy yourself with *her*!"

The thought of leaving Jude is daunting although the break will probably do me good. I have never been one for gallivanting on holiday anyway. I prefer to relax by the pool and chill out. He has nothing to worry about – I wish I could convince him.

***

After a few hours of sulking, Jude has come to terms with being alone for a week and asked me to spend the night with him before I go. Of course I am still apprehensive, although overjoyed at the thought. I must make a plan. I will tell Charlie that Pandora is ill and wants me to stay with her. He will believe me because it happened once before. How exciting and scary!

September 9th

We had lunch yesterday and all was well – not a crossed word. Things are definitely moving up a gear and Jude's mood has been great this past week. Only six days to go until Italy. Boy am I going to miss Jude! My night with him excites me more than the holiday. *I wonder if we will have rumpy-pumpy at last*? Every time we meet, I think this could be it and then nothing happens. I always shave my privates into an immaculate landing strip and floss my teeth until they squeak – just in case. Thankfully, I have lost weight (a bit too much really.) At least my muffin-top, bingo wings, floppy tits and cellulite have gone. My appetite has been a bit off these past months, so I tone up with simple exercises. I am forever prepared. *Will the inevitable happen during the second week of September*? I have no fucking clue to be fair.

September 14th

What a magical night I had expected this to be! I sang at the top of my voice all the way to Jude's house. The car window was wound down, with the radio blasting and the air was filled with sweet-smelling anticipation. I wore a long flowery dress with red shoes and had curled my hair into rows of little flicks. As I stepped out of my car, Jude came to greet me at the door as always.

"You look absolutely stunning, Cathy."

I just smiled coyly and ran to his arms.

He took me for a delicious meal. We touched hands and laughed so hard throughout. Everyone stared at us. I wondered if we looked as beautiful to them as we did to me.

As soon as we returned home, we rushed through the front door. Jude firmly shut it behind him as he forced his tongue into my mouth. It was pitch-black but we had no inclination to find a light switch and happily fumbled about in the dark. He cupped my breast and squeezed it until it hurt. I made a whimpering sound which caused him to quickly let go, but I took his hand and returned it to my heaving bosom. His other hand hungrily searched for my crotch as I simultaneously tried to find his. His cock was rock-hard and rather large, if I may say so – I was ravenous for it. We both laughed as he pulled me backwards toward his bedroom. He pushed me onto his bed and threw himself on top of me. He was heavy and I was happy to be crushed if necessary, just to experience this wonderful act I had patiently longed for.

He gently rolled my dress straps down past my shoulders, then stood up and went to the end of the bed. He pulled the bottom of my dress with such force that I laughed – it reminded me of a magician with his tablecloth. We were like a couple of Eskimos, who are renowned for laughing during sex apparently – I read it somewhere. Now I was in my underwear – thank God the lights were out. However, what we looked like was of no consequence to be honest. It was dark and we *felt* beautiful. His cock was pressed hard into my stomach as he began to awkwardly remove my underwear. First he took off my bra and to my joy, my boob was positioned in such a way, that it appeared quite pert – I think the edge of the pillow had conveniently propped it up or something. He licked my nipple and then bit it hard – it felt fucking brilliant! Then he fumbled down below and managed to remove my knickers – I kept laughing nervously, though he was undeterred and even sniggered himself a bit. It was lovely and felt so right. He was in his underwear by now and asked me to take them off. Call me old fashioned but I have always found that so lame, especially if they ask. I pretended not to hear so he just whipped them off himself.

I kept thinking, *'I hope he can manage it with those bloody hips of his.'*

"I love you, Eloise," he said, as he touched my most intimate part very softly.

I had waited so long to hear those words and my dream had come true. He gently slid just the tip of his finger inside me which made me shudder.

"I love you too, my darling, more than I have ever loved anyone. I would be happy to die right now, Jude. It's perfect ... I want us to be like this forever, but we won't will we? Why can't life always feel like this?"

Jude stopped caressing my fevered body and sat up.

"You feel the same as me, don't you, Cathy?"

"How do you mean?"

"You find something good and it always goes rotten."

"It does seem that way, doesn't it?"

"Why don't we end it then, Cathy – together?"

"Don't be absurd, Jude, I was being theatrical," I answered; now feeling very silly and quite nervous.

"No, no, don't get me wrong, Cathy. I was caught in the moment and thought it was what you wanted to hear."

I lay very quietly as I heard him pull his trousers on. He put on the light and had a look of devastation on his beautiful face. "You don't love me at all and now I've lost my hard-on."

"I do love you, Jude, don't be silly. I'm sorry; it's just that sometimes I'm not sure how to take you. Please don't be cross."

"Let's go and have a cup of tea, Cathy."

"How British!" I said, trying to lighten the mood – not even a hint of a smile!

At first, I wanted to go home. However, after an hour of drinking tea and talking, Jude became more relaxed and we began to laugh again. We went to bed eventually and he just kissed me goodnight on the forehead and turned off the light. It was a huge disappointment, but we were okay and proper intimacy is bound to happen one day soon. Anyway, we slept together in his bed and held each other all night which was really nice.

September 21st

I arrived back from Italy this morning. It was a lovely holiday but I missed Jude like mad and am eager to see him just as soon as I can. It was horrible not having the internet so we kept in touch daily by text. In fact, I have just counted the texts and we must have exchanged over three-hundred. He is dying to see me too. I do hope he trusts my behaviour abroad. I know he worries, which is sweet, *but what is there to worry about*? He just hurts himself with his thoughts. I hardly left the villa.

Pandora

Once again, Eloise and Jude were in each other's arms. As September drew to a close and autumn set in, they carried on with their strange affair and I heard very little from her. All she spoke of in Italy was him. She remarked that although they were sexually active in their teens, her memory was blank. Even when she read her old diaries, she had no real recollection at all. I found that quite odd and wondered if something awful had happened that she needed to forget. I had certainly heard their noisy passion on the night of their meeting. Perhaps it was something later on. This sexual amnesia haunted her. She said it may as well never have happened. I think she wondered if she would *ever* experience the thing she had only seen in a photograph.

Chapter 8
Murderer

October 2nd

In Italy I found a wonderful market that sold lots of old artefacts – the sorts of things Jude loves to have on his wall. I bought him a small ornamental stiletto sword. It will sit so well amongst his eclectic collection of new and old pieces. They range from ancient African carvings to religious works of art – and then there are the guitars and Wurlitzer. He has a neat but contradictory style which rather reflects his state of mind. There was also an engraving stall at the market. It sold those keyrings with a broken heart. Both halves of the heart were magnets which held them together. I had the stallholder engrave Cathy on one half and Heathcliff on the other.

Charlie is going on a sixth form trip to Norway next week and will be away for two nights. Jude has asked me to make the most of my freedom and stay with him for at least one of those nights. I will give him his presents then. We have had a couple of lunch dates which were hardly intimate in a busy restaurant. I want us to be alone when I give him his gifts. He has been a little aloof since my return but this could be his way of trying to punish me. This time I force myself to have no expectations at all. It could move our relationship up a notch or it may just be a pleasant fun evening. I will not allow myself to get carried away with my thoughts. Jude has been fairly calm recently and free of woe for the most part. I still have my doubts about us and sometimes tell myself he is mad. I want to help him however ... if I can. *What if he is mad? What if I walk away? What if he commits suicide or something awful*? Mad or not, I still love him and there is nothing much I can do about that – at my age! Honestly, I should know better and throw in the towel. All of this is such hard work!

October 7th

I stayed with Jude last night...

I arrived around 7.30 pm pruned and tidy, like a sheikh's wife who had been scrubbed and delivered to his tent. I remained stoic with my intent to expect nothing. However, preening and scrubbing had become par for the course, so I went through the same routine out of habit – *or did I*?

"You look gorgeous, Cathy, how do you do it?"

"Just a bit of slap and some clothes … you know!" I lied modestly.

Jude cooked some steak and then he put on a DVD for us to watch. It was some boring old film, starring David Niven, about a fighter pilot who dies and goes to heaven, whilst the lady radio controller, to whom he last spoke, tries to bring him down to earth from limbo – or some such crap. I think Jude hoped it would put me in a romantic mood but I just fell asleep across his legs. Suddenly I was awoken by his hand frantically searching down my knickers. I was shocked and, quite frankly, in two minds by now. It felt good however and I quickly made him aware of my consciousness. I wondered why he had done this whilst I was sleeping. It was fairly rough and frightened me a little. I pulled myself up and sat beside him. He looked into my eyes and his looked rather empty and cold. Then he put his tongue inside my mouth and kissed me brutally. My feelings were a mixture of excitement and fear. He stood up and pulled me forcibly through the hallway towards his bedroom. I found myself caught in the moment, confused and obedient. *Was I having a lucid dream? Did I really want this after all*?

He threw me onto the bed with such a force that it hurt. I had never imagined Jude being the 'rough sex' type because he had always treated me with respect before. He has often been saucy but very romantic with it – and that is why I loved him. Now I am unsure of how I feel. This was very different and not what I had expected at all.

He tore at my clothes with such frenzy, that my blouse was ruined. All the buttons popped off and I remember thinking, '*He'll bloody well pay for a new one.*'

The elastic on my underwear burned my skin as he ripped them off at break-neck speed. He groped my breast with one hand and tore at my vagina with the other. His fingers felt like barbed wire, ripping me inside with his nails. He keeps them long for his ridiculous guitar strumming – but I aint not fucking guitar!

"Jude, you're hurting me, slow down!" There was no reply.

He put his mouth to my most intimate part and his tongue was as long and fat as any cock. This was a bit more like it and there was no pain. I welcomed his ferocious gluttony although it shamed me to. I felt as though I was having sex with a complete stranger. But it was Jude so I was obliged to comply. Not exactly willing … obliged.

Then it happened. He took his cock (which was now the size of a small canoe) in his hand. He thrust it inside me and my head began to spin. It felt good, but it was somebody I had never known – not Jude after all. He pushed his hips so hard, that I swear his cock was almost into my ribs. His sweat was pouring onto my face and naked body as he grunted and moaned. I looked at his face and it was twisted into a demonic grimace. *Where was Jude*? Then he came and let out an almighty scream. His claims of extended celibacy were likely true because it was over quite quickly. I felt a warm surge that seemed to go on forever.

During this performance, I had been quite still. I did nothing much in the way of reciprocation because I was in a state of bewilderment. I lay in silence. Jude went to the bathroom muttering something about my lack of response.

"I can hear you, I'm not that deaf! You just took me by surprise, that's all."

I had a little tidy-up and then got dressed. I went into the lounge, where Jude was sipping hot tea. There was a cup for me on his mantelpiece. I took it and then awkwardly sat beside him.

"I've got you a little something from my holiday, Jude."

"You shouldn't have bothered, I don't deserve anything."

"Don't be silly, I was waiting for the right moment to give it to you, it's in the car, I'll go and get it."

He opened the stiletto first and just said. "That's nice."

"I thought it would look good on your wall."

"Yeah, but how on earth did you get it through customs?"

"I just put it in my case, why do you ask?"

"It's a real blade; you can get done for that."

"You're kidding; I thought it was just an ornament."

"Well just count yourself lucky you didn't get caught."

I felt sick at the thought of breaking the law without realising. *How stupid am I? Whatever would have happened had I been caught?* And he seemed quite unimpressed with it – adding insult to injury.

"I'll put it on the wall behind my bed with my two small carvings; I think they come from Italy."

Then he opened the keyring and burst into tears.

"What's wrong, Jude?"

"No one has ever bought me anything like this before."

"It's only a keyring."

"But the thought that must have gone into it! I don't deserve you."

"What makes you say that?"

"I want to end it all, Cathy. I am bad. I have done bad things and now I've ruined our relationship."

"What makes you think you've ruined it?"

"I've defiled you and made you the same as every other slut I've fucked. I wish you'd stopped me."

I was aghast. *Did he really think this or was it just another game?* He rarely showed any guilt or remorse. If this was another mimic, it was a bloody good one.

"Well perhaps we'd better lay off the sex for a while if you aren't in the right frame of mind, eh?"

"Don't patronise me, Eloise."

No use arguing alert!

I finished my tea and started to gather my things.

"Where are you going?"

"To give you some space, I think you need it."

"No please stay. No more funny business, I promise... just hugs and sleep, besides I need to tell you something."

"What?"

"I know you love me and I can trust you, so it's time to tell you the truth."

I sat and listened, expecting the usual mumbo-jumbo. However, I was about to be mortified.

Jude had worked as a driver in the late eighties for some pretty dodgy characters. He would often don a dress-suit and ferry them to and fro, thinking he was simply a chauffeur at first. I knew something of this, but if Jude's claims are true; I have been barking up the wrong tree entirely. He was involved with gangsters and was sometimes their getaway driver. On one particular occasion, they robbed a post office and the proprietor was shot dead. Jude was horrified by this and said he never expected any casualties. He heard the gunshots and waited anxiously for the criminals to get back into the car. He sped through the streets in a state of shock. As he entered a junction, in his fear and panic, he hit a child on a bicycle. He wanted to stop but his boss told him to carry on driving. They got away and were never caught or brought to Justice. Shortly afterwards, Jude read in the papers that the boy had died and, of course, he blamed himself. He told me he was granted permission to leave the firm soon after, which was customarily unheard of, but he had gained their respect because of his obedience. He had acquired a spinal and hip injury – likely from the traumatic car journey and shock of it all – he would no longer be of use to them anyway. The criminals were eventually imprisoned for subsequent crimes and Jude remained a free man.

"You can't change what happened, Jude, and you are repentant so try to forgive yourself."

This was probably the most insincere thing I had ever said to him. I had no pity. I was repelled and just wanted to go home. If it *was* true and he had put his trust in me, I should tread carefully. He could be dangerous. If it was a lie, then he is totally mad anyway.

I said very little after that. I thought it best to stay and play out my part in the game. He spooned me all night in his bed, but things were different now. I kept myself awake the whole night and remained very still. I looked at the wall and begged for morning to come. I needed to get away...

October 8th

I am an emotional wreck. I am shocked, tired, frightened and above all, I feel like such an idiot. I will have to try and think of excuses to make myself indisposed. I cannot see him... I need time to think... Oh God, What is Pandora going to say? I had better avoid her for now. This is far too much for anyone to digest.

Chapter 9
Cat and Mouse

November 3rd

Keeping Jude at arm's length is my best option right now, all the while trying not to rile him. He thinks I am down with the flu. He is still whining on about how I put everyone before him which is completely untrue. He is forever at the forefront of my mind although not for the right reasons at the moment. I think I still love him which means I am just as sick as he. He can probably sense there is something wrong, though neither of us have mentioned *that* night.

I have also been keeping things from Pandora lately so feel quite alone. She is my closest friend and the only person I can trust. I feel bad keeping secrets from her. She has always kept my spare house-key and now has the one to my desk – I gave it to her after our holiday. Charlie and Frank must never have access to my desk. If they ever find out what I get up to I will be dead meat. Even my laptop and phone are impenetrable with bizarre passwords. I told her that if I get run over by a bus, I want her to read my work or even try to get it in print. Agents and publishers are still rejecting me but I shall persevere – writing helps me focus and cope with Jude. I remarked that books and paintings always seem to fare better posthumously. Pandora gave me such a serious look and I just laughed. Making wills and plans during one's middle years are simply a practicality...

***

This morning at 9.am Jude sent me this:

For my Cathy
Twenty five years ago, two single, beautiful but sad and lonely people, happened to meet... They fell for each other and love was born. But due to the insecurities of one of these beautiful people,

they separated, seemingly never to see, smile, touch or love again. That was until they happened to meet once more through a very strange coincidence. They met, they spoke and they touched again. They were reminded of long lost emotions and even lost love. Stunted by the pain they had both suffered, they sought solace with each other but some battles and scars take a lifetime to heal. Both these beautiful souls carried too much pain...

One particular perfect day, these two souls met and walked through the stunning beauty of togetherness, holding hands like lost children. They laughed as they strolled through fields of peace, clutching each other for comfort. On that day, one of these souls realised he was in love ... and was smitten by her beauty and her smile.

But something was wrong, because beneath the perfect exterior on this wonderful day, was an undercurrent of unhappiness and pain... They agreed that now was not the right time to be together but one day, in the not too distant future, they would again be one. It would be 12/07/2013. They had tried to rush this inconclusive love but, again, the stirrings from their past brought many tears and pain.

There was a time when a promised phone call was lost in the stinking mire of rejection and hurt... Someone felt unwanted and unloved ... and that was me, Jude. But unbowed, I promised to stand at the back of the queue and wait ... and this sentiment remains...

This soul will wait for you, Cathy ... but will not suffer any more pain. And neither should you. This soul has tried to love, understand and be there for you when you fell. But extraordinarily, it was not as important to you as it needed to be. It felt hurt and unwanted. It was not the most important soul any longer.

The ending of this short story has yet to be written. The future lies in the hands of Cathy and Heathcliff. One soul prays that one day they can be together ... and that soul is mine.

But this soul cannot take any more pain... as it has already been stripped and beaten red raw with lost love and rejection. Let these souls just touch each other's hearts during this waiting time, by exchanging words of love and true feelings. If this is not possible ... then they must set themselves free....

If we truly love each other, we will find true happiness in each other's arms, rather than around the noise of those who hate, with the petty jealousy that surrounds them. We are, after all, allowed to fall in love...

Sent with tired eyes ... an aching heart and much love, in the hope of a better life in the future ... together...

Heathcliff

***

Well, to think I once fell for this hyperbolic turdiness... and why all the bloody buts and dots? (Sorry ... ellipsis.) I have had cause to edit the shit out of this, to make it even readable – and as I mentioned before, I am no expert. I left the dots for a laugh however. It could have been quite beautiful had it been real.

The way he talks of the lost love from our teens baffles me. Only last week he got into a huff and said I had simply been one of his 'shags.'

November 5th

Guy Fawkes Night. How boring! I am trying to get on with my life and my writing, although it is never easy when I hear an email ping every five minutes. I should turn the volume off. It would make no difference actually. I would probably keep checking them anyway.

Good God, look at this garbled nonsense:

I don't think you are ready for a relationship with me... I said you were too busy with too much going on in your head... You agreed... I said let's give ourselves time... We agreed... Then you just disappear and don't even talk with me... Or you tell me you're with your family when you aren't... You were with fucking Pandora weren't you? Make up your mind, cunt!

One hour later… (God, these dots are catching on.)

Just got in… Been to gym… whoooooooohoooooooo! And then shopping… boooohoooo! And now I'm eating cheese on toast… your favourite! And I'm not bothered what you do on wankbook and who you talk to… Why would I, you cunt! Ha ha! … I just noticed you were posting at 3am… when you should be in bed, thinking about me… I will ring you in 10.

xxxxxxxxxxxxxxxxxxxxxxxxxxxxxxxxxxxxxxxxxxxxxxxxxxx

Holy shit! I will have to go to the shops. My mobile can stay here.

November 6th

I have just about managed to avoid Jude and this morning he has messaged me again. I am in no mood to rewrite his embarrassing crap; so instead, I will regale the message briefly. He has bought me a framed, signed copy of the Kick Inside album by Kate Bush apparently. He took great pleasure in telling me it was an early Christmas gift which cost him £300.00. Of course I would love to own it – if he is actually telling the truth and not playing silly buggers. But I cannot face him yet. I will continue to make excuses until I am ready to claim the prize I deserve. I know! I will say I fell and broke my hip.

November 8th

He's not bothering me as much now because he thinks I am suffering. I had a curry delivered last night with a little note saying, 'love Jude, and hope you feel better soon.' It made me feel really bad. *Why should I feel guilty?* He has brought the whole thing on himself with his lies and moods. Perhaps I could have overlooked his murky past if he were not such a liability. He has given me nothing but grief for the past nine months.

***

The doorbell just rang and it was Interflora with a huge bunch of red roses and a giant teddy bear. I will have to hide them in my bedroom. It is getting rather crowded in there now with all his stuff. I might need to have a bit of a clear-out.

November 20ᵗʰ

Jude's stalking is still ongoing. Sometimes I think it is sweet and that he is really trying to make amends. Other times it unsettles me and I wonder how this will all end. I still have feelings for him, only now I realise he is probably beyond help. Perhaps I will try just once more and advise him to seek psychiatric support. I will suggest he sees a proper psychologist, not an idiot who can be easily duped. I am hell bent on keeping my distance until early December at least but I want that bloody album, if indeed it actually exists. Maybe we can meet for a coffee in safe territory and I can put my psychologist idea to him.

November 24ᵗʰ

I can no longer be bothered to even bore *myself* with all the messaging and piffle exchanged daily. The longer we are apart, the less I miss those days with Jude. But I will never be able to forget them.

November 27ᵗʰ

He may have taken the hint now. I get the odd message, asking how I am and it feels safe enough to politely reply. I had never felt that way about any man and I doubt I ever will again. It would be nice if we could be just close friends but that would be difficult. He needs someone to keep an eye on him.

I have good days and bad. I can function without that terrible heavy feeling of hurt now. My feelings are definitely changing. I am stronger and glad that I avoided being dragged into another hell. It is hard to let go completely. It would be odd to never hear from Jude again. Sometimes I feel like I want him gone from my life completely. Other times that notion seems impossible to imagine. He is harmless as long I keep my heart closed and my hand on my halfpenny. Perhaps I was wrong about it being a game. After all, there could never be a winner. His only enemy is himself. Perhaps he is far too damaged for human interaction. I sometimes wonder if he is suffering the effects of Foetal Alcohol Syndrome. I have read about it. In fact, I have read about a lot of psychological disorders since I met Jude... Poor Jude!

Chapter 10
Gifts

December 3rd

Jude has been distant but polite for the last week or so. I have received a few cordial messages, asking after me, along with the usual self-pitying rhetoric about how lonely he is. He emailed this morning and asked if we could meet in a café, halfway between our homes.

'Can we meet up because I have something for you?'

'If you like. Perhaps this Friday lunchtime?'

'Great. See you in the Northolt car park.'

My apprehensions and feelings are conflicting. It has been a month since our last meeting and my life has begun to function normally again. If I hear a song on the radio that reminds me of last summer, I still have those feelings of passion and adventure which I miss. I still worry about Jude because although he is a madman, I am his only friend. I know he is tormented and wonder if he knows how he tortures me. I often think it is deliberate and selfish although part of me wants to believe he cannot help himself. He is an enigma and I have to see him just once more. I need to understand before I can surrender completely to a life without him. It will be safe in a public place because he will never create a civil display and will undoubtedly play the perfect gentleman. It will give me the opportunity to be daring and advise him to get some help. Without it, his life will always be in turmoil. He will never develop legitimate friendships, so remain alone forever. After all my internet surfing and reading about sociopathic behaviour, I realise that, if he indeed does have these tendencies, he's not very good at it. These people do a far better job of hanging onto their victims than Jude. *What am I saying? He still has me worrying about him, even bewitched in a way.*

So I am off to meet him in one hour.

December 4th

As I pulled into the car park, there was no sign of Jude's car. I found a bay quite close to the entrance, and as I attempted to brake, my Ugg boot got caught between the brake and accelerator. Bloody automatics! It was impossible to stop. As I tried to turn my foot toward the brake, it continued to accelerate and I crashed into a metal fence. As I reversed, the same thing happened. The car sped backwards and it was lucky there was no one walking behind me or I would have squashed them. *Was this a bad omen?* I managed to pull the handbrake up and just sat with the back half of the car jutting out of the bay. The front was smashed and I began to cry. Then I saw Jude knocking on the window. I opened it and he smiled.

"What have you done, you silly cow?"

"I don't know." I was sobbing uncontrollably.

He opened the door and took my hand.

"Get out and I'll park it properly, then we'll see about getting it fixed."

He parked the car whilst I stood, looking like a complete tool.

"Come here, Cath, give us a hug."

He held me so tight and I thought, *had I been the car, that hug would have put all the broken bits back together. He did have a heart. That was real – it had to be!*

We walked to a steak house and I told him I had no appetite after my ordeal.

"We'll just have some tea and croissants then, I want you to have something, you're in shock, my darling."

For a while, I just sat and watched his mouth move. He was not short of conversation at all and acted as though we had never been estranged. I heard nothing of what he said and just nodded every so often. After a while, I felt a little easier and ate half a croissant and took a few sips of tea.

"You are so thin, Cathy. What have you been doing to yourself, where are your boobs?"

That did make me chuckle.

"Why don't you use a megaphone and ask the whole shop," I said, and by this time I was laughing.

"I want us to be the way we were, Cathy."

His beautiful, cheeky smile stole my heart and his gentlemanly conduct had me smitten all over again. Selective memory was jading my logic.

"You hardly know me really, Jude."

"Yes I do."

"No, I pussyfoot around you all the time. I can never be myself. I have to be on guard with you and bite my tongue constantly. I don't sing in front of you or fart; things I always do around people I'm truly comfortable with. You hardly know me at all. You don't love me; you love someone I pretend to be. Someone that doesn't exist."

I could hardly believe I had blurted that out. I needed to say things I had never said before and thought this was the perfect opportunity. He seemed to ignore every word, as if they were of no consequence. *Does he think it is good to have someone who cannot be themselves and simply dances to his tune?*

"I want you to come back to my house so we can talk more. I need to get back for the dogs soon."

"I don't know, Jude. Perhaps it's not such a good idea."

"Well, we can drive back to mine. Your car is only a bit dented at the front, and then I can find someone to fix it."

"I don't think I want to drive, I'm too scared."

"It'll be fine, come on. I've got something for you in my car."

We walked back to the car park and he got into his car, summoning me to get in beside him. Then he gave me a huge parcel.

"This is for Christmas, but I want you to open it now. I probably won't get to see you at Christmas, what with all your family commitments."

I was pleasantly surprised because he was usually rude and resentful towards my family, and then he went and spoiled it by saying, "Next Christmas we can be together because your son will be gone and you can tell the lot of them to fuck off."

My reasoning, that hung by a thread, told me this event would be unlikely. I remained silent as I opened my present. I was aghast. It was the singed Kate Bush album. I had decided it was probably bullshit in the end and forgotten about it.

"Look at the back, Cathy."

I turned it over, and attached to the back of the frame was half of the heart I had given him months before. It was the half engraved with Heathcliff.

"I didn't expect this, Jude. I don't know what to say."

"But I told you about it ages ago."

"Yes, but things have changed since then and I've only got you a CD," I said, as I handed him the small parcel.

"Don't be silly, it's fine."

We drove to his house.

It was the strangest feeling being back there. I felt the ghosts of Jude's dark moods and the violent sex. I also felt the warmth, the love, the excitement and the feeling of being home, albeit the strangest home in the universe. It was our world.

He led me to his room which was pristine with a brand new duvet set and candles. I realised that this had all been planned. Did I care? Yes and no. Was I flattered? Fuck, yes! He lit the candles and started to undress. He lay on the bed with a hard-on that I can only describe as majestic. His tanned, ribbed body had the most beautiful glow I had ever seen. I wanted to melt into it and disappear so I would be forever part of him. After awkwardly removing my clothes, and wishing I had Jude's talent to fall out of them with ease, I climbed on top of him and felt the tiny beads of sweat that adorned his gorgeous frame. I eased myself onto his cock and slowly moved up and down as he groaned. He held my breasts as I pushed slightly faster although not too much. I wanted this to be passionate but tender. I leaned back a little and reached out my arm to touch his balls, gently stroking them which is something I have always been good at. He could scarcely feel my touch because of its subtlety, but he knew it was there and the impact was more explosive than any clumsy grope. It sent him into convulsions until he was fit to burst. He pulled me towards him and kissed me fervidly until my face was on fire. His stubble rubbed and ripped at my cheeks and I welcomed his magnificent devouring tongue. I pulled myself free from his huge manhood and lay beside him. I grabbed his thick curly hair and pushed his head toward my most intimate part, greedy for his tongue. It darted in and out and then entered me so deeply that I let out a scream. Then he bit my fanny, not too hard but enough to source the biggest orgasm I had ever experienced. He then sat up and smiled a smile that I will remember to the grave.

"It's too late for me to fuck you, Cathy," he said as he put his cock hastily into my mouth and instantly filled it with so much spunk, I could hardly breathe.

My mouth was full and there was nowhere to spit it out. Reluctantly, I had to swallow. I hate that.

It was wonderful and I was happy once again. We got dressed and Jude carried out his usual tea-making ritual. As we drank our tea, I could hardly stop myself from grinning. I know he is nuts so I decided to just live in the moment.

"What are you grinning at?" he asked, smiling wryly.

"Just happy, that's all."

"Yes, and now you will toddle off home and leave me alone again."

"Well I have things to do, I'll be back soon."

"I wish you would move in with me."

I had no intention of arguing but felt I had to stand my ground this time. We were properly intimate now and I could no longer pussyfoot around him.

"Yes, Jude, but what happens when you need your alone time and have your dark moments, would I have to move out every five minutes?"

"Don't be such a nasty bitch."

"I'm not. But it worries me. Can't you see your doctor or something? It can't be nice for you feeling so down all the time. I want to help you. Why don't you make an appointment? I'll come with you if you like."

"There's nothing wrong with me. It's you."

"Look, Jude, let's not spoil a nice day. It's just some of the things you say. They don't make sense. It frightens me when you talk about us ending it all and stuff. You blow hot and cold all the time. I just want us to be happy and we can."

He was angry; I could see it in his face and began to wish I had never gone to his house. The look reminded me of the time he attacked me in our teens. I had to get out of there.

"I want another shag," he demanded.

"What, already?"

"I've got enough pent up frustration to go on all night, Eloise."

Now I knew he was annoyed with me. I was no longer his Cathy, just plain old Eloise. He pulled me from the chair and his grip was strong. I tried to free myself but to resist was impossible. He dragged me along the hall and back into his bedroom. He threw me onto his bed and then tore off my trousers and underwear. I tried to pull them back up as he removed his own. He slapped my face and I kicked him in the shin as hard as I could. My attempts were futile as he pinned me down by my arms. He pushed his half flaccid penis inside me as his erection was failing – which made him even more psychotic. He withdrew and tried to force the big wobbly thing it into my mouth which remained firmly shut as I punched him in the stomach with my free hand. He gave up and pulled on his clothes, then tutted as he left the room. I quickly got dressed and fearing for my life ran from the house. My hands were shaking and clumsy as I tried to find the ignition of my battered car. Soon the engine roared and I quickly drove away.

***

I can hardly remember the details of our sex-life when we were young. I dare say Jude has difficulty recalling it also. But that is likely because he was on drugs and had a succession of women before and after. I should be able to remember – he had only been my second lover. I thought perhaps I was approaching menopause and my memory was failing. It bothered me and maybe that influenced my eagerness to have sex with Jude again ... hoping the memories would come back to me. I always imagined it to be something beautiful. It pains me to think it was no such thing ... perhaps it was always like this...

I have a curious feeling that Jude will see this as just a lover's tiff. I have no idea what to do now. I think I have been raped ... I am definitely not going to tell Pandora.

December 12th

I am numb. I am alone. Jude has not been in touch. Perhaps that is just as well. Christmas is coming, Kate Bush is under my bed, my keyring is in my knickers drawer, my bumper is fixed and I have never felt so unhappy, stupid or wretched in all my life.

Chapter 11
Shrink

January 10th 2013

Happy new year ... not! My journal has been gathering dust for a while. I cannot find the inspiration to write. Perhaps I have been burying my head and wishing it would all go away. My feelings are blunt. It is though I am in limbo with a sense of nothingness. I am starting to believe in solipsism. No one else exists at the moment. When I go outside, people seem to be rushing past with nothing in their heads. Am I the only one to suffer? Is other people's suffering real. Is Jude's suffering real? Is Jude real? I have been to my doctor and explained how I feel without going into detail about Jude. He says I have had a breakdown, coupled with a condition called derealisation. I am on a course of antidepressants and need to see a counsellor regularly. In just a few weeks, I have gone from feelings of shock and confusion, to feelings of hurt and now to this...

Christmas was like an animated ritual. I thought I may as well spend it with the dreaded ex, Frank because Charlie wanted him there. I hardly cared. I cooked and opened presents with a bogus enthusiasm, all the while feeling like death.

To my shock, Jude texted me on Boxing Day, asking why I had ignored him over Christmas.

'You know I'm on my own but you couldn't even be bothered to give me a ring and wish me happy Christmas.'

I chose to ignore it.

Now I am hell-bent on keeping him out of my life for good. It will be hard because he knows where I live. I can ignore the texts and emails but I refuse to change my number – I have had the same one for ten years. He has my address however, so I must find somewhere else to live. I hate this house anyway.

Charlie dashed into the house briefly one afternoon and I told him we needed to move.

"I have found a lovely little flat in Barnet and it's much cheaper than this big, old, cold place."

"Oh, Mum! I don't want to move, all my friends are here."

"It doesn't matter, I've got the car and can run you wherever you like. It's only six miles away, for God's sake."

My fuse is beginning to shorten with Charlie. He is going to university this year and when he comes home, he will do his own thing anyway, like teenagers do. It is simply somewhere to hang his hat. I can see his father in him now and I need to set boundaries and be in charge of my own life for once.

My new flat is warm and cosy, right by the shops in a friendly neighbourhood. I am unable to get the keys until early March and it needs a lot of work. Pandora thinks I am moving because I fancy a change and it suits my budget better. She is going to help me decorate as soon as we get the keys. Meanwhile we have bought paint and new flooring which is cluttering up my lounge like you would not believe. At least when I am gone, Jude will never find me.

I went to Pandora's for coffee and we swapped ideas about how to style the new place.

"Where have you been hiding, Eloise? I haven't seen you in weeks."

"Well it took me ages to find a flat that I liked and what with Christmas, Charlie and everything…"

"Have you fallen out with Jude again? You rarely mention him these days."

"We're still in touch, but the romance side of things died ages ago."

"Sorry to hear that," was her curt reply. Her gratification was not easily hidden. I felt so guilty telling her lies.

So now I must wait for the move. Stressful as it is, I look forward to the change and it gives me something to focus on. I had better start packing some boxes…

January 17th

Jude has been texting, calling, emailing and generally being a fucking nuisance over the past couple of days. I knew he would be back eventually. Full of apologies about his moaning text at Christmas and telling me that our sex session was a thing of beauty, including the second attempt presumably – Jeez! I have decided to send him one last email and that will be it.

'Jude, you are sick. I have gone easy on you because of this; otherwise I would have had you arrested before Christmas. I want you to leave me alone. I don't want any more contact with you or I will get a restraining order, I can promise you that. What you did was tantamount to rape. I would suggest as a friend who, for some bizarre reason, is still concerned about you, that you get some help and quickly, before you woo another woman and destroy her life. I think you may have sociopathic tendencies and if you don't get treatment, you could find yourself in prison sometime soon.'
Eloise

His reply came pinging back faster than ever before. I had to read it and fully expected a plethora of expletives and insane ramblings.

'Cathy, you have taken the whole thing the wrong way. You clearly took charge during our first fuck. I liked that and wanted to go again – this time with me being in charge but I had nothing left to give. I'm not getting any younger, you know lol. I thought you were just playing along and wondered why you left the house like that. It was rude and that's why I've been a bit off with you. That was all it was, my darling. Sorry if our wires were crossed.'
Jude x

Jesus Christ! His talent for words is phenomenal, and his capacity to turn the whole thing onto me is extraordinary. I refuse to offer a reply to that load of balls. It was my last email to him and that still stands

January 21st

At 2 am this morning, I received a text from Jude.
'I'm at Edgware General Hospital. I've taken an overdose.
Jude x'

This is a tough one. It is now 9 am and I feel wracked with guilt. *Does he really believe that his actions were appropriate?* I suppose I had better go and see him.

***

He looked terrible as I approached his bed. He gazed up at me and sobbed.

"I can't believe you called me a rapist. My heart is broken."

"Are you going to be alright?"

"Yes, they pumped my stomach but I wish they hadn't."

"Look, let's just get you better and we'll get some help for your depression."

Depression was my polite term for psychosis, a word that would have surely sent him over the edge.

"Do you really think I need to see a shrink?"

"Well someone like a clinical psychologist then. Some of the best of us have seen them," I answered, with a faux, reassuring smile.

"Okay then, you win. If it saves our friendship, then I'll do it. I think I have to agree to some sort of therapy anyway before they let me out."

Friendship? What drugs had they given him?

"Will you come with me if I have to see a shrink, Cathy?"

"Yes, of course!"

***

What the hell am I letting myself in for?

Is it just guilt on my part? Can he be saved? Does he really believe he is incapable of rape? I have promised now, so I suppose I must go with him to his doctor. However, no more sex or even the slightest hint of romanticism, and certainly no more visits to his house.

January 23rd

Jude was released from hospital this morning and I picked him up just before noon. We collected medication for his 'depression' from the pharmacy and then I took him home. He has been given weekly appointments to see a clinical psychologist. I hope they get to the bottom of this for both our sakes. During my studies of all the mental maladies that exist on the internet, I am sure the best course of treatment would be depression and anti-psychotic medication. I am no doctor but, boy, is Jude one depressed psychotic human being! He blatantly refused to take his meds years ago – he said he hated the way they made him feel. Well if they *are* prescribed, he had better bloody well take them now.

He asked me to come inside as I stopped by his drive and I made excuses not to. The hurt was visible in his often dead eyes and I felt really bad.

"I have a doctor's appointment myself in half an hour," I lied.

"Okay then, maybe next time." Then he kissed me on the cheek and got out of the car.

I waited until he was safely indoors before driving away. He made no enquiries about my own bogus appointment. He is unaware of my breakdown and there were no sessions scheduled for today. Had he asked, I would have been unable to lie convincingly anyway. I was shattered and in no mood for games. He rarely concerns himself with my wellbeing. That is just Jude. Me me me me me…

January 25th

Many pleasantries have been exchanged over the last couple of days and Jude has clearly been checking his behaviour. I have insisted we are just close friends now, as the sexual thing did not work out (to put it mildly) and he seems to be going along with it for the moment. He says he wants us to have lunch each Wednesday after his sessions with the doctor. I have agreed because we will be in public places, and I am safe as long as we are never alone. Jude still has no clue I am moving house or have to see a shrink myself once a week. How did I get into this drama? Oh yeah, fucking Facebook…

Chapter 12
Andy

February 6th

Jude and I continue to talk by email or phone on a daily basis. He simply chats away, nothing too heavy and still seems to be on his best behaviour. He has an appointment with his clinical psychologist today and I shall be driving him there. It has all happened rather quickly so I presume the hospital doctors are concerned about him. He is clever and manipulative however which worries me. I hope this psychologist is not easily duped. Oh well, best be off.

***

Jude declined my offer to accompany him into the counsellor's office. I know from experience that you are entitled to have someone with you. This has made me uneasy because I have no idea what was discussed. Jude told me he regaled his unhappy childhood (again) and gave her an outline of his feelings and moods. Her name was Eleanor and he kept on and on about how lovely she was. I can just see him trying to charm the pants off her. It sounds plausible; although I am worried he may have been economical with the truth. He needs to be honest about his aggression, mood swings, sexual peculiarities, and those crazy suicide pact ideas. I'll bet he mentions none of that. Without the whole truth laid bare, everything will be out of kilter and a bloody waste of time. He came out of the office looking a little tired and confused but quite upbeat.

"How did it go?"

"She reckons I've got Post-Traumatic Stress disorder and need at least twenty counselling sessions. She's a bit hot," he beamed.

"What medication did she prescribe?"

"She told me to continue with the antidepressants."

I did an imaginary eye-roll and thought. *At least he's doing something.*

Jude suggested we try a new restaurant for lunch. He had eaten there before and said it was very good. He was quiet during the meal and just grinned at me every so often. We had never experienced uncomfortable silences before so I tried to make conversation.

"Do you come here often?"

He fell about; laughing hysterically, yet I had been perfectly serious. I realised how funny it must have sounded so began to laugh with him. We both laughed until we cried in the end. The ice had been broken and we began to talk of all manner of things. We had a lovely time and, to other people, must have looked so happy. Jude obviously needed to steer clear of the mental health subject. With much sadness, I decided that this was going nowhere.

I drove him home and he kissed me on the lips as he left my car. My passion for him was still very much alive as was his passion for himself. There was no invite to come in which left me relieved and disappointed at the same time. Perhaps he sensed my distance although empathy has never been his strong point. He will undoubtedly try to woo me again when the fancy takes him – I know the pattern and I know his games.

All we can ever be is friends now. There will always be that elephant in the room and he is not taking his counselling sessions seriously. I am too afraid to challenge him so all I can do is drive him to his appointments once a week and perhaps have lunch. I will have to break the tie sooner or later. Enough is enough.

February 12th

Jude continues to message me once or twice a day. Usually just to say hello and tell me how he feels, and then goodnight around midnight. I always send a friendly reply.

Being Jude's friend is hard. It would be easier if I were indifferent but I doubt that will ever happen. There is a huge hole inside me where our love used to live. Before I met him, I was happy being single. I wish our paths had never crossed again – this emptiness is too painful.

My heavy heart has driven me do something slightly mad. I know from experience that one gets over loss eventually. This time however, I doubt that will happen. Something has to fill this dreadful void. I have signed up with a dating site – something I used to laugh at. I would call those people sad and pathetic; having to look for love on the internet. Jude came back into my life that way, but it was Facebook and an accident – *or was it? Did I push too hard? Perhaps I was lonely back then without even realising.*

From the moment I joined the ridiculous site, I have been bombarded with pings and friend requests. Many of the men are sweet and lonely, telling me my picture is gorgeous and asking lots of questions. I am shallow and vain. Ugly old men do nothing for me. I want a Prince. I am such a horrible person. I will probably delete this stupid account.

February 14th

It is Valentine's Day and Jude has sent me a card. I thought it best not to send him one and feel awful now. I sent a message of apology and he told me not to worry which made me feel even worse.

Yesterday I found myself looking at the stupid dating site again. I got talking to a man named Andy. He said he was lonely and recently divorced. I told him very little about my love life, or lack of it, and simply said I was single. He was unlike the others. He was dark and handsome which made me very wary. *Why would someone as gorgeous as him be on a dating site?* I wondered if he were some sort of pervert who picked up women on the internet as a hobby. Or even worse, was married and looking for bits on the side. He chatted away for a good hour and charmed me no end to be honest. I was careful about what I said and gave him no contact details. He said he lived across the opposite side of London to me and owned a gym. He was keen to meet me for dinner and gave me his mobile number. I feel excited and scared. If I text or call, then he will have my number which could be a bad idea. I will wait for a couple of days to decide. The weirdest thing of all is he looks like Jude.

February 16th

I have caved in and texted Andy this morning. I just said, 'Hi!' and he replied, saying, 'good to have your number, must meet up soon.' – Yikes!

Perhaps he is genuine – I do hope so. All of this is a welcomed distraction from Jude.

***

Andy rang this afternoon and we had a long chat. I felt at ease with him and there were no awkward silences – always a good sign in my book. He told me he has three sons, who all work at his gym. He is living with the eldest until his house, where his ex wife still lives, is sold. He has a nice voice; a little bit cockney but warm and smooth as silk. He wants to pick me up and take me out for dinner next Friday. I am glad because there is no way I would drive through London, especially in a state of nerves.

February 19th

Andy rings me a couple of times a day now. Jude's whinging hellos have become more of a background noise. I am taking him to counselling again tomorrow as promised and will keep the subject of Andy firmly under my hat. Jude would be furiously jealous, even though he constantly gives me the cold shoulder. He has never really treated me like a proper girlfriend.

February 20th

After Jude's counselling session, which you can bet was an Oscar winning performance, we went for a pizza. I have lost interest in his manipulation of doctors now and he can just get on with it. I am simply doing him a favour.

"You look a bit fed up, Cath, anything wrong?"

"No, I'm just a bit tired."

"Are you still writing?"

"Yeah, trying anyway, not that I think anything will ever get published."

"Don't be so down on yourself, you are a great writer."

This was a proper 'Eddie Murphy staring into the camera moment.' After all the insulting things he has said before! What a nutter!

"Yeah, well, I'll plod on." I would have laughed at the irony, but my energy to do even that had expired.

"Have you been seeing anyone, Cathy?"

"What do you mean?"

"Have you met a bloke, is what I mean," he spat, with eyes like the devil.

"No, don't be so silly," I lied.

"Good. You will always be my girl, you know that don't you? Just give me time to sort myself out. I would kill myself if you left me for someone else."

"Okay."

February 22nd

My date with Andy is tonight and I am scared shitless. Although this takes my mind away from Jude, perhaps I am stupid getting involved with someone else. *Maybe he will find me repulsive. What if his picture is about twenty years old and he is fat and bald with a beer-belly?*

***

Andy picked me up around 7.30 and took me to a smart restaurant this side of London. He was chirpy, chatty and looks just like he does in his photo, so that was a relief. I ate nothing all day, hoping my appetite would be good and not stifled by nerves. It was fine and I ate like a horse. We talked and laughed all the while like old friends. He drank water because he was driving so I did the same. He is a genuine guy – I am a million percent sure of it.

"Do you want to come back to mine, Eloise? My son is away for the weekend. Not that I will try anything on," he stuttered. "I just don't want the night to end yet."

"But it means a lot driving for you, Andy."

"No, it doesn't matter, I shouldn't have asked," he said.

He clearly thought I was rejecting him as his face flushed with embarrassment. I took hold of his hand.

"I'll come back with you, Andy. That sounds really nice."

I was comfortable with Andy right from the start and felt I could trust him. I had every intention of having sex with him – even if it was just to flush away the past eleven months. He is a man and was bound to try.

And try he did. We had coffee with posh little biscuits and he played some soothing music. His son's home was immaculate and I liked that. It was very modern and minimal, unlike Jude's.

Soon I was led upstairs to a beautiful room. It was warm and fresh, without the smell of dogs. He took off his clothes and lay on his bed, beckoning me by patting the empty side. It was evident he was an ardent workout freak. I suppose it makes sense if he owns a gym. His body was beautiful. Jude's body is beautiful but leaner and his skin is much darker. I was unafraid and brazen as I removed my own clothes and joined him. We made love very gently for almost an hour. He was sweet, tender and an excellent lover. I realised I had never *made love* with Jude. My lack of emotion was disappointing. I hid it well however, with a resolve not to hurt Andy's feelings.

We cuddled for ages and then I fell asleep for a while. As I awoke, Andy was dead to the world and still holding me softly. As I looked at him, all I could see was Jude. I shook him lightly until he opened his eyes.

"I have to go now, Charlie will be wondering where I am."

"What's the time?"

"2.30."

"Blimey, I'm sorry, I'll get dressed."

"Don't apologise. He'll be expecting me, that's all. I don't usually stay out all night." – *I thought I would get that in...*

The drive home took over an hour but we had plenty to chat about. I told him all about Pandora and how alike we were.

"Aw God, don't tell me there's another one of you knocking about," he quipped.

We were still getting to know each other to be fair, and I wondered if I would ever see him again. Did he think I was a slapper, shagging on the first date? Then we arrived at my house although I got him to stop a few doors down, in case Charlie was spying.

"Well, thanks, Andy. That was a lovely evening."

"No, thank you! Can we do it again in a couple of days, or is that too soon? I don't want to push it."

Another Eddie Murphy moment! That was the last thing I had expected.

"Umm, well, perhaps next Friday again? Charlie's in sixth form and I have to be up early to drive him to school on weekdays."

"That would be lovely, Ellie."

Ellie? I wish he would call me Cathy.

He kissed me on my mouth and then I got out of his car. I turned to him and smiled.

"I know this must sound stupid, but I think I love you, Ellie."

My smile became broader. "Night, Andy."

As I opened the door, I heard Charlie snoring. It was a relief – I was not up to the third degree.

Andy is a lovely man and so gorgeous to look at. I am very flattered and should think myself lucky. I wish it could have been like this with Jude.

Chapter 13
Moving

March 4th

Andy and I are getting along famously. What a pleasant change to have a decent man in my life! We talk every day and he makes no obsessive demands on me. He is aware of my problems with Charlie and his dad. He has a rational grip on the situation and understands we have to be careful until Charlie goes. I feel guilty keeping Jude a secret from him. *What other choice do I have though*? We had another date on Friday and it was fabulous. We went back to his house again and through the motions of pleasant, if not overly passionate sex. It is nothing like sex with Jude and I wish it could be somewhere in-between. Sadly, again there was little emotional connection on my part and the earth hardly moved – it simply wobbled slightly. Anyway, it looks like Fridays will be a regular thing from now on.

***

I drove Jude to his appointment last Wednesday and then to a pub for lunch. This time he was different. *Was the counselling actually having some effect or was it just another game?*

"Cathy, I'm feeling so much calmer and content, I think we might have cracked this thing?"

"We?"

"Yes, we. If you hadn't insisted on me getting help, I would probably still be in torment."

He did look a bit brighter and the dead eyes had a certain sparkle.

"Charlie will be off to uni this September, Cathy. That's only a little over six months away. I know I was impatient and grumpy but it's gone much quicker than I thought it would. I think we can give it a try and have a proper relationship."

"Perhaps – let's wait and see how it goes."

I had to play along. It just came out of the blue and threw me completely.

March 6th

Today I get the keys to my new flat and Jude still knows nothing about it. I have told Andy and he offered to help out. I thanked him and said that it was all under control. I no longer want to be a damsel in distress type; I want to be more like Pandora. At last we can get cracking with the decorating. My old neighbour is laying new wooden floors and Pandora will help me paint, hang new curtains and generally titivate – she is expert at that sort of thing.

I told Pandora about Andy a few days ago. I can hardly keep it to myself. I am spending so much time with her now, besides we need something to talk about. She always makes me nervous and thinks my taste in men is dreadful – well it is I suppose. Sometimes her judgmental attitude gets me down although this time she is pleased for me – she says he sounds like a nice chap. However, she knows nothing about my weekly meetings with Jude. She thinks that was over weeks ago.

A new cooker, fridge and washing machine are on their way as there are no white goods in the flat. The old house is packed up so the worst is over. I hate packing and downsizing – the stress is like nothing else. Now this will be the fun part but hard going nonetheless.

The work will begin tomorrow and should take around a week. It is a bit of a rush job because I need to get out of the house quickly. Two lots of rent payments are tough on the old bank balance. We should have started today and I have to take Jude to his bloody appointment and listen to more of his bullshit.

***

Well that was fairly painless and I just nodded as Jude held court and spoke of our future together. I have no idea how to tell him it will never happen.

***

March 7th

Frank has been giving me a terrible time with his incessant shouting down the phone. He reckons I am moving to upset Charlie and drive him out of the house so I can entertain men. Absolute rubbish! I want a place that is affordable and without memories of that bully. I always told myself I would never bring men home with a child in the house and have stuck to it. Besides, Charlie will be gone in a few months for much of the time, although this will always be his home. Frank insists I should have remained in that old damp house for Charlie's convenience. Frank is a control freak and furious at my putting more space between us. It will be harder for him to check where my car is. He would kill me if he knew what was really going on. He has literally been screaming at me almost every day for the last month. But the deed is done and I have made decisions on my own – he hates that. Now he is making it his mission to badmouth and turn Charlie against me – and it is working. I feel so bullied and depressed. I sometimes wish I had parents to turn to, but they were always worse than useless anyway. Thank God I am so busy; otherwise I honestly think I would end it all.

***

The decorating is underway and my moving date is planned for Saturday the 16th. I have hired a van and offered my neighbour some money to drive it. I asked Charlie if he and his friends would like to help, and said I would pay them. He has refused so I will have to ask elsewhere. There are plenty of people looking for work so it should be easy enough. Stress has caused me to become even thinner than usual. I weigh just over seven stones and look dreadful. I must have aged ten years in these past few weeks. Lord knows what Andy sees in me. My appetite has always been good but worry burns calories. Now I have no urge to eat at all, making matters worse.

Well, must crack on with the decorating. I am meeting Andy again tomorrow night and I am exhausted.

March 8th

After a hectic day at the flat, my dinner date with Andy was a welcomed break.

"Get that down you, Girl. There's nothing of you," he said, as he watched me play with my food.

"Do I look horrible then?"

"No, you look gorgeous as ever, just a bit tired and ... well ... thin."

"It's all this moving business. I'll be fine once I get back into a routine."

"Will you carry on writing?"

"Definitely! I'm tweaking the first one now and already have ideas for a second."

"That's great!"

"Yeah, I suppose. Even if I only sell a couple, at least I would have contributed something to the world."

"Don't look so sad. You have a son and you're very artistic and clever."

"I suppose."

I began to cry a little back at his house, after trying really hard not to. Then I opened up about Frank.

"One day I will catch up with that cunt and punch his fucking lights out."

***

Feeling sorry for oneself is not an attractive trait. As I sit in alone, surrounded by boxes, I simply want this day to be over. Poor Andy! He is so kind and always touches me with a gentle strength. There is never innuendo, teasing or games. He is what he is and leaves nothing to the imagination. Perhaps I am a bad-boy magnet and secretly enjoy torment and goading. I am certain Andy would see me every day, given half the chance. Perhaps he views my indifference and lack of demands as sweetness and patience. Maybe he thinks I am simply cautious and well-grounded. If only he knew the truth. He seems too good to be true sometimes and I wonder if he is also on the rebound. At least he appears devoted – unlike me. I wonder if he really loves me. I am always someone else around him so Eloise is a fake – *or is she?* Perhaps this is the real me after all. Restraint and patience can be learned and Cathy needs to become Eloise again. I could work on it and make a go of things with Andy– if I can find the sense and energy. My miserable face was undoubtedly obvious to him tonight. It must have been like shagging a corpse. An ironing board would have had more enthusiasm and I certainly look like one. Jude is always lurking in the back of my mind which is so unfair. If only I could love Andy back, everything would be perfect. I could run away with him and be done with. The best thing is to give it time and hope that this happens. Otherwise I need to do the right thing and finish with him if – for his sake.

March 12th

Working on this bloody flat is wearing me out. Charlie has done nothing to help and we finished his room first. This was to pacify him; although why I indulge the brainwashed child is beyond me. To be honest I would rather he saw it finished than in its present state. He would be sure to tut and look down his nose. I have kept in contact with Andy and he is sweet as ever. Tomorrow is Jude's counselling day so I must take time out from working. I still get a funny feeling before I see him, rather like a fix or something. I doubt I will ever get him out of my system completely which is depressing.

March 13th

Well that was something I could have done without.

Jude's behaviour has improved these past weeks and I did not expect such histrionics this afternoon.

He was extremely quiet as we drove to his appointment. I asked what was wrong and he said his back was hurting and he was tired. He went into the counsellors office with a face and then out again with the same look of woe. We went to the steakhouse and he hardly said a word.

"Come on, Jude, tell me what's wrong."

"You're moving and you didn't tell me."

I felt sick. I hardly use Facebook anymore so it was never publicly announced. *How on earth did he find out?*

"You've gone very quiet, Eloise," he said, with a sarcastic snarl.

"Look, Jude. You had enough on your plate and I only got the keys a few days ago. It needs a lot of work and I didn't want to bother you about it. I would have told you when it was all done and dusted."

"Yeah, right!"

"Of course I would. I haven't even moved yet. How did you find out anyway?"

"I was thinking of renting my house out a few months ago, to move to a smaller place, nearer to you."

"I had no idea," I answered, still feeling sick and none the wiser.

"And guess what? The estate agent sent me the details of your house yesterday!"

Shit!

"That's a coincidence," I answered, desperately trying to imply nonchalance.

"Hmmm it is. So I never even got to see where you lived."

"Look, I've told you a hundred times that would be too difficult. You said you were prepared to wait until Charlie was gone. At least the new flat will be a home I've never shared with another man and you'll see it soon enough." I thought that might shut him up for a while and we could just get through lunch.

"Where is it anyway?"

"Berkhampstead." The lie just rolled off my tongue.

"Not too far I suppose, but I'm always at the bottom of your priority list, aren't I?"

Then I lost it. "No, you aren't. You're being impractical. Maybe we haven't seen each other as much as we'd like these past months but you have always, every fucking day, every fucking hour, every fucking minute and every fucking second been right at the top, in front of everyone else, embedded into my fucking brain like a fucking parasite. Don't you fucking get that?

He stormed off and must have taken a bus home. I sat as the tears rolled down my face, out of my nose and into my mouth. Suddenly I noticed many eyes upon me. I had made a show of myself and not even noticed those around me. They had heard everything and thought I was mad. Well I am. I picked up my bag and walked out of the restaurant.

March 15th
My Friday date with Andy was pleasant enough and, as usual, I went through the motions. He now believes that when Charlie leaves home I will be his – Just like Jude did. Jude is ignoring me and I doubt he still wants me after last week. I should be relieved but it hurts. The flat has taken longer than we thought to finish; there were some leaks to deal with. I am moving tomorrow with the help of Pandora and a couple of neighbours.

March 18th
Charlie and I are settling in now although he complains about the place at every opportunity, and I am sick of hearing it. He went out for the day when I moved, and turned up later that evening with a look of disdain as he toured the flat. His father is clearly egging him on; it is almost like listening to that bastard. We still have a few boxes to unpack and loads of stuff ended up in the communal bin. I would have tried to sell it but have no energy at all. The man from BT has installed my internet properly this morning, as it was on the blink. I was lost without it. There has been no word from Jude and I suppose he will be taking himself to his appointment on Wednesday – if he bothers to go at all. I reckon it was simply a sham to humour me.

March 21st
Still busy, busy, busy which is just as well. It takes my mind away from the sadness and gloom. I think Jude has dumped me once and for all. He messaged me yesterday and said he would be taking himself to appointments in future.
'If you want to be my friend, Eloise do keep in touch.'

'Okay, if that's what you want.'

'To be honest, I'd prefer the friendship thing. You haven't been looking well lately and being so thin has aged you. I don't really feel the way I used to.'

Ouch, that really hurt. I wondered if was playing games again or perhaps he really meant it. I was so upset it was hard to let it go. Maybe it was simply a great big dent in my ego.

'You don't fancy me anymore?'

'I don't want to hurt you, Eloise, but no, I don't. I'm sorry.'

My upset was getting the better of me and for the first time in ages, I wore my heart on my sleeve.

'You don't just go off someone like that. Not so long ago you talked about us moving in together and everything. I don't understand.'

'I'm sorry, must dash. I have to take the dogs out. Speak later.' (No kisses.)

***

My heart is broken and it makes me realise I will always love Jude no matter what. Deep down I had never given up hope of us being together one day. *Why did he say such hurtful things*? If I had gone off *him*, I would have let him down gently. That was so cruel if he is telling the truth. It will be too difficult to face Andy now. I must phone him and cancel our date. In fact I must tell him we are over.

***

Andy says I have broken *his* heart. Pandora thinks I am bonkers and wonders how I could let go of such a catch. I have nobody now and it is my own stupid fault.

March 23rd

Late Thursday afternoon, I must have left my emails open when I popped into the kitchen. I am usually so careful. I was confronted this afternoon by a very hostile Frank. I opened the door and he looked at me with hatred in his eyes. He barged his way in and pushed me into the lounge. He put his face close up to mine and began to yell.

"You have been seeing a bloke, haven't you?"

I was bewildered and afraid, so just answered, "No."

"Charlie saw your email to someone called Jude. It was pathetic! You were begging, and asking why he didn't fancy you anymore— you stupid, gullible tart."

"He's just a friend, but he's got mental health problems and says weird things to me."

"You're well suited then. So what was all that shit about you moving in together?"

"He asked me ages ago and I refused. I just wondered why he'd changed his mind. It was only an ego thing."

"I suppose he found you on the internet. You really are a stupid woman. Have you had sex with him?"

"No, we've never met. You know I'm not a highly sexed person."

"No, you're a frigid cow."

"I've been feeling awful lately, what with you shouting at me and Charlie looking down his nose. I needed someone kind to talk to."

"Well he didn't turn out to be all *that* kind did he? How long has this fucker been grooming you?"

"He hasn't groomed me; I enjoyed the attention and we were only friends, but obviously not anymore."

"Well do what you fucking like from now on, you stupid cow. I'm out of here. It's a shit-hole anyway."

Frank stormed out of the flat and slammed the door behind him. I have no idea why I acted like such a coward. I should have stood my ground and said it was none of his fucking business. I should get a restraining order and tell him never to contact me again. I only give him the time of day because of my son. Charlie looked at me and said he was sorry.

"I just thought Dad should know, that's all. You're vulnerable and men take advantage of you."

"That's your father talking, Charlie. Don't patronise me. I know I've made some stupid choices, and your father is certainly one of them. You're all a bunch of fucking hypocrites. But you don't have to worry; I am done with the lot of you.

"You are better off on your own, Mum."

"Fuck off, Charlie."

Chapter 14
Published

April 4th
My book has kept me busy these past couple of weeks. I have edited and polished to the best of my ability. At least it has kept my otherwise muddled mind occupied. I submitted to a publisher on Tuesday and was surprised to get a very prompt reply yesterday. They are reading the full manuscript as I type, so my fingers and everything else that is crossable are crossed.

Both Jude and Andy have left me alone completely. Not a word from either in almost two weeks. In one way I like it, in another I am consumed with loneliness. Anyway, now is the time to start work on my second book. All the crap I have endured this past year has held me back. Perhaps being single is what I need to make something of my life.

Charlie continues to skulk around and has started drinking in nightclubs. He phones me at all hours to pick him up at the weekend which is exhausting.

I am pretty sure that Frank encourages it. I can just hear him saying. "Get her to pick you up; it's her fault you had to move."

I did promise to ferry him about but he takes the piss somewhat.

So, there is nothing much to write about at the moment.

April 24th
My book will be published towards the end of July. Yayyy! I am terribly excited and quite shocked to be honest. The publisher says that she loves it and thinks it is easily marketable. The story tells of a woman's traumatic trials in life which she overcomes with strength of will and character. Most of it is based on my journals, though I am still looking for my own happy ending. The tale concludes as she separates from her controlling husband. Perhaps one day I will write another book about Jude – I have enough material, for sure. Anyway, back to work.

April 26th

This morning I received an email from Jude.

'Hello, Cathy. Sorry I've been quiet for a while. I'm writing another children's book, so that's kept me pretty busy. I'm sorry we had words and hope we can still be friends. It feels weird without you in my life. xxxxx'

***

It has been almost a month since we argued and I thought it was the finish of us. I am taken aback now. He has done this before and always made contact towards the end of his four week sulk. I remember counting the days and panicking as it got closer. His pattern has always been the same, though this time it was unexpected and I had stopped counting.

I will have to think about this...

April 28th

My second book is rocking and I am really enjoying it this time – probably because I am making it up as I go along with much of this last year thrown in. I am taking all the nice bits from my diaries about me and Jude. It will be the perfect love story – just the way I want it to be – such fun and it makes me feel better about it all.

I am almost embarrassed to write this down, but I met Jude this afternoon. He messaged me non-stop for two days so I caved in and replied. He wrote he was keeping up with his therapy and doing really well. He constantly apologised for his behaviour and it sounded genuine for once. There was something quite different about him this time. He is always more pleasant face to face but now he even sounded joyful as he wrote and the self-pity was gone.

'I realise how lucky I am and how much potential there is in my life. There are many people far worse off than me and I'm ashamed of the way I treated you. Like a fool, I drove away the very best thing of all. Please come and see me. xxxxx'

Never before had I heard such positivity from Jude. His acting ability and games are clever and I have been fooled many times. But this sudden lack of self-pity has thrown me. He seemed to enjoy wallowing in martyrdom before and had no control over it. Perhaps that is changed now and a breakthrough has been made at last.

I drove to his house after cooking lunch for Charlie and arrived early in the afternoon. He stood in his doorway, as I pulled into the drive and I have never seen anyone look so happy.

"I've missed you so much, Cath."

He hugged me until I was breathless and I liked it.

Then he put his mouth to mine and kissed me tenderly. He had never kissed me this way before and I liked that even more.

We sat in his lounge drinking tea and I could hardly get a word in – though I was relieved in a way because I had no idea what to say.

Eventually I did butt in, "How's therapy going?"

"Great thanks. She could see I wasn't making much progress, so she put me onto cognitive behavioural therapy and medication for mood-swings."

This pleased me no end because it was exactly what I thought he might need in the first place. Was he learning to cope, behave and live a normal life, or were his sessions just acting lessons? I forgave myself for the cynicism and hoped he was telling the truth.

"Will you stay for tea? I'm making cheese on toast?"

"Yes please, that sounds nice." (Fuck me; we've turned into Darby and Joan.)

The afternoon was a lovely one. I took a big chance on going and am glad that I did. We talked about old times, laughed about the charging bull, the shouting in restaurants and we held hands a lot. There was no sex – I think we should take baby-steps in that department.

I am happy, excited, wary and terrified all at once. *Am I insane?*

April 30th

Yesterday I visited Jude again. He is keen to see a lot more of me now, and daytime is good when Charlie is in school.

As soon as I entered his house, there was tea and toast on the coffee table. We chatted for a while and then he asked if I would go to bed with him. I had really wanted to wait a while but the temptation was too much.

We walked into his room hand in hand and sat on the bed. It felt a little uncomfortable as if we were strangers. I suppose we were in a way because this is a new start for us. We got undressed and lay in each other's arms for a long while. Our warm naked flesh melted into one – it was like a dream. I could feel his cock was hard but he did nothing for ages except kiss the top of my head.

"Shall we make love, Cathy?" he whispered.

"Yes."

For the first time he made love to me properly. It reminded me of Andy which upset me a little – poor Andy! Jude was sensual and gentle this time. He kissed my body all over before gently putting his cock inside me. I could feel his heartbeat close to my own but also in his throbbing penis. It felt big and beautiful and I almost climaxed, then suddenly he gently withdrew. He lowered himself down to my lulu which was already saturated by the smooth rhythm of his enormous dick. He licked and sucked until I came into his mouth. It was the best orgasm I have ever had in my entire life. I doubt it could ever be surpassed.

"Now I can die," I said, giggling.

Suddenly I wished my rhetoric had stayed where it belonged – safely inside my mind. *Why had I blurted it out*? I remembered the last time he had taken it literally.

Hastily changing the subject, I put his cock into my mouth and blew him until his glorious juice spewed forth – then I had to swallow it again – Yuk, I wish he had a spittoon by his bed. I am not generally a swallower!

"That was amazing, Cathy."

"The best!"

***

I arrived home in time to pick Charlie up from school.

"You look happy, Mum."

"I am, Charlie. The writing is going well and this time next year, we could be millionaires!" I joked, sporting my best Delboy twang.

Thoughts of my secret rendezvous are still sending chills through my entire being. There is such warmth in my chest – like that sensation you feel after a glass of Baileys. Or even the way people describe sensing the Holy Spirit, like a fire in your soul. The fact that my son and his father know nothing makes me smug. My plan is to wait until Charlie has gone in September and then go public with Jude.

I would love for bullyboy Frank to come knocking at my door, and for Jude to open it, saying, "What do *you* want?" Ha ha!

We must err on the side of caution however. I do tend to get carried away easily. If I plan too far ahead it may go horribly wrong again – just one day at a time – though they do say optimism is a good thing. I have read *The Secret* and will attract positive vibes from the universe. Do I sound happy? I should do, because I am...

***

I have set boundaries and told Jude my book is important and needs attention for at least six hours per day. If I fall backwards, allowing him to consume my life again, I will have worked for nothing. A balance is needed. I think that has always been my problem – no symmetry in my life.

I need to catch up today – perhaps we can meet again tomorrow for a while.

***

My publisher has just emailed. She has read the synopsis for my second book and wants to commission that as well. Life is on the up!

Chapter 15
Love and Lies

May 4th

Writing is keeping me busy and I find it most therapeutic. I make time to see Jude however, and took a day-long break yesterday which I thought was well deserved. I told Charlie I was spending the day shopping with Pandora. I see very little of her nowadays as she thinks I am too busy which made her the perfect alibi.

Jude and I spent the entire day together. We went shopping, walked the dogs and then back to his house in the afternoon. We listened to songs on the Wurlitzer and even had a slow dance to 'I'm not in love' by 10cc. This, of course, was the perfect precursor for us gliding instinctively to his bed. Once again the love making was the perfect equity of tenderness and passion although he spoiled it a little with his coarseness afterwards – as if he were somehow undervaluing what we have.

"You give the best blow-job, Cathy. None of the slappers I've had can top that."

I felt uncomfortable and told myself not be so sensitive. I tried to reciprocate in a similar, humorous vein.

"And you do things to my hoo-ha that no one else could," I replied, having heard the phrase mentioned somewhere.

Finding a fitting term for my lady-parts has always been difficult. Some of the words people use are vile. My attempt at half-hearted merriment paid off. Jude howled with laughter and said I sounded like Al Pacino having a fit. His quick wit always astounds me. He makes me laugh but sometimes things feel sordid and dishonest.

He cooked an early dinner of Salmon, fresh vegetables and a nice chilled bottle of non-alcoholic wine. He said alcohol made him sick because of his medication. I suddenly realised we have never drank alcohol together this time around. Even when we eat out, he always orders soft drinks and never keeps booze in his house. I had given it little thought as I try to keep my consumption to a minimum anyway – it turns me into an idiot. We used to knock it back by the gallon as teenagers, even without food. It is probably a wise thing in retrospect – it makes Jude loopier than a loop and could perhaps trigger his recreational drug habit again. He had set the table beautifully with flowers and candles. My appetite has returned with a vengeance so I had no trouble tucking in. Afterwards we had profiteroles with ice-cream.

"I suppose I'll have to go soon and cook for Charlie."

"Can't he make himself something?"

"Yes, of course he can but I like cooking his tea."

Jude's face spoke volumes. The old resentment was still there and his ongoing jealousy of Charlie made me uncomfortable. I did understand in a way because we all feel a bit jealous at times – human nature I suppose. I tried to change the subject.

"How is the therapy going?"

"Great thanks, can't you see a difference in me?"

"God, yes."

The rich food gave me a rumbling stomach so I headed upstairs to the bathroom. I normally use Jude's downstairs toilet but was afraid of sounding like a brass band in full thrash. After my ablutions were concluded, I noticed a row of pills on his shelf. I had a bit of a peek to see what he was taking. Everything seemed to be in good order, until I saw the labels were dated early April. It would appear his prescriptions are repeated monthly, so the bottles should have been almost empty. I walked back downstairs with a heavy heart and kept quiet about it.

"Well I really must be off in a minute, Jude."

"Okay, but we must do this again soon."

"Of course."

"Then when Charlie goes, I can come to yours for dinner."

"That would be lovely."

"Where do you live exactly? You haven't told me yet."

"I'll write it down in a minute."

Something had stopped me from telling him – though I was unable to fathom out why.

Then my phone rang. '*Shit*,' I thought.

I always turn my phone off before going to Jude's house and yesterday I forgot. I was too complacent. He was my real boyfriend now and my head was somewhere else. Somewhere it had never been before. I was forgetting to be careful and forgetting how to be devious.

I looked at the screen and it was Andy. We had ceased contact weeks before and my face must have told a story.

"Who's that?"

"Oh, it's just Charlie wondering where I am."

"You look like you've seen a ghost. Who the fuck is it?"

"Charlie." I was scared and it must have shown, as I rejected the call and snapped the flap shut.

Jude snatched the phone from my hand and opened the cover. I tried to take it back but was overpowered by his strength and anger.

"Who the fuck is Andy?"

"Just a friend."

"You've never mentioned him before, and why didn't you answer him then?" he yelled. "You're fucking him, aren't you?"

"No, I'm not!"

"I'm gonna ring the cunt and ask him myself."

"No, please don't. Okay, I'll tell you the truth."

He threw the phone against the wall and sat with his head in his hands. I sat opposite him and tried to explain.

"It was when we broke up and I didn't have any feelings for him. I was lonely and tried to love him, but just couldn't. All I could think about was you. Please believe me, Jude."

"Did you have sex with him?"

"Yes, and that's all it was."

"Did you like it?"

"Not much."

"Not much? I want you to say you hated it."

"OKAY, yes, I did, I hated it."

"I'll kill the fucker."

"Well you were leading me a dance and it's not his fault."

"Fucking sticking up for him now, are ya? Oooh lovely Andy, we can't be upsetting Andy, can we."

There was no point in arguing with Jude. He was hurt and angry and I needed to go before he completely lost it. I got up from the chair, when suddenly he leapt towards me and put his hands around my neck. He pressed his fingers hard into my throat, until there was no more air. His face was contorted and evil. At that moment, I remembered his attack in our teens and, again, thought it was the last thing I would ever see. Then everything was black.

Several minutes later, I awoke on Jude's couch.

"I'm so sorry, Cathy, please forgive me."

My throat was sore and I could hardly speak.

"It's okay, I shouldn't have lied. It's my fault." I tried to sound convincing and just about pulled it off. I had to get out of there.

"Please don't leave me, Cathy."

"I won't. You know I'll always come back, don't you Heathcliff?"

It was time to get away and never return to this lunatic's house. He is a master of manipulation and has taught me well. I had learned the perfect technique and the right words to manipulate right back at him. Perhaps I am as bad as he with all the lies and exploitation. Andy knows nothing of Jude and Jude knew nothing of Andy until yesterday. My circumstances were extenuating but a liar is a liar and I am the worst of all. My only comfort is that I have never resorted to violence.

As I entered my flat, I quickly found a jumper that hid my welt marks and then, blinded by my tears, shamefully cooked Charlie his long awaited dinner.

* * *

Much of my evening has been spent surfing the internet and reading about various psychological tendencies, particularly those of psychopaths, sociopaths and narcissists. There are many tests so I took several on Jude's behalf – just to be sure. He ticks almost every box perfectly. He is totally self-absorbed. I need to be certain and to get him out of my system completely.

* * *

Profile of a narcissistic sociopath – Charming, manipulative, grandiose, lying, authoritarian, secretive and divisive. Enjoys having control over his victim and gets a thrill out of making them doubt themselves. *He is incapable of love and empathy.* That fits Jude perfectly. The grandiose part reminds me of his delusions or artistic genius. He is a very good photographer and extremely poetic with the spoken word but his grammar and writing are not so wonderful. He insists that he is the best author ever and publishers would happily print minor errors because of his artistic licence. He reckons his talent is such; he is entitled to break the rules of writing anyway. He also believes he plays guitar like Jimi Hendrix but all I've ever witnessed are painful and squeaky noises.

People usually become wise to sociopaths eventually. I can hardly believe the number of forums where victims seek advice. Their stories are so like my own. I had my suspicions fairly early on and knew something of the subject. I read a lot about psychiatry and should have seen the signs. Maybe I did and simply put it to the back of my mind. Perhaps I hoped my concerns were silly and mistaken. How had I missed all this before? Was I deluding myself too? Many people had been fooled by their sociopaths for years. Was I lucky this had only lasted for one, or is Jude just stupid and incapable of maintaining his own psychosis? Sociopaths are supposed to be clever but, like anything, it is not a one size fits all disorder. Maybe that was what threw me. Jude has not been taking his pills – well not this past month anyway – that is a certainty. His therapy has certainly had an effect, although not the intended kind. Behavioural therapy is of no benefit to a psycho. It simply teaches them how one is supposed to behave. He may as well have gone to the Italia Conti stage school and be done with. It was just a means to an end for Jude. But it has backfired on him big time. Suppressing his real feelings has worsened his temper so it is time to give up. I have tried and tried with him for way too long now.

May 5th

This morning I phoned Andy and thought it was time to explain why I ignored his call – and everything else. My mind and my lies are a sickness that has consumed me for far too long and I needed to cleanse my soul or something. I told him all that has happened during this past year and he was very understanding. He was hurt that I slept with him whilst still loving Jude and was baffled by my adoration of a nutcase. I told him it was over because Jude tried to strangle me.

"Whaaaaaaaaaat? I just called to say hi and ask how you were. I'm so sorry I put you in danger."

"It's not your fault, Andy. If I hadn't told so many lies and used my brain a bit more, it wouldn't have happened."

"Where does the cunt live?"

"No, I won't have you getting into bother over him. He'll dig his own grave soon enough."

"Did you ring the police?"

"No."

"Why not?"

"I don't know. I just want to forget about it."

"He might do it to someone else. Ellie."

"I doubt it. He never gets that far with women usually. I'm the only idiot who stuck around long enough."

"Did he hurt you badly?"

"I was out cold for a while and I've got a really sore throat but I'll be okay."

"As long as you're alright. Don't have anything to do with that bastard again – you promise?"

"Yes, I promise."

Why is he so damn sweet and why am I unable to feel anything for him?

"Do you want to meet up again? You might not love me but we can have a good laugh."

"Okay, I'd like that. Can you give me some time though? I need to get my head straight first."

"Alright. We'll still keep in touch, yeah?"

"Of course."

I love Andy but not in the way he wants me too. Having him as a friend right now is invaluable. *Why do I run to men to take shelter from another?* I do it every time. I was bullied by Frank and ran to a man I thought was my saviour. My saviour transpired to be a lunatic so now I will probably be on my own or run to another unsavoury loon. Perhaps I can grow to love Andy. Who knows?

May 16th

Andy rings me every afternoon now. We only have a quick chat and then back to work. I have been keeping myself busy with the book and am going great guns. I wrote a farewell letter to Jude a few days ago.

'Dear Jude.

You know I loved you and probably always will but it can never work between us. I know I lied and so did you. I noticed your bottles of pills were still full and your attack on me was unforgiveable. You are emotionally unwell and I just hope you get the help you need and deserve one day. Otherwise you will always be alone and that upsets me a great deal. Ideally, I would love to keep up to speed with how you are doing, although it only seems to cause hurt for both of us. I wish you the very best from the bottom of my heart. Cathy x'

Deep down I know he is likely beyond help now. However, a line needs to be drawn under this chapter of my life. It hurts like hell as my year with Jude draws to an end. It seems so much longer than a year, but now I realise nothing more can be done. I am exhausted.

May 26th

My second book is almost finished in first draft form. It has become rather more sombre and dark than I had first intended and evolved into a love affair that goes horribly wrong – mine and Jude's story, in fact. I have gone back through it and been more honest. It has depressed me no end so I hope my publisher likes it. It needs some fine tuning and I wish to have a happy ending with

Andy. We shall have to see. If there is no happy ending, I will simply invent one. I have been really busy and am having a rest today. There has been no reply from Jude which is a huge relief. Today is Pandora's birthday and she is throwing a party this afternoon. We had almost lost touch for a while and I wonder what I should tell her. Oh, she will be far too busy entertaining – enquiring after my shenanigans will be the last thing on her mind – hopefully.

It was a good party and I casually mentioned I was going out with Andy again soon.

"Oh good. I really like the sound of him. Why didn't you bring him?"

"He's having lunch with his kids today."

"Oh shame. Still, he sounds like a nice family man."

"Yeah. It took me a while to get to know him, but he's alright. She laughed.

More lies. Pandora would go to Jude's house and kill him it she knew. Perhaps I will tell her the truth one day when we are alone – if she has a couple of weeks to spare.

May 31st

Jude has not replied to my letter which suits me fine. He must know his true colours have been exposed; therefore I am no longer of use to him. He will feel no remorse – I realise that now. He may be afraid of repercussions, although that will be all he feels. Everything is about him.

I took the plunge and went out with Andy tonight. We had a lovely meal and he brought me home straight after. He is trying to woo me slowly – I can feel it. He must love me, especially after what I put him through and I am frightened. I never want to lose his friendship although I know he wants more. I worry that I will be a huge disappointment to him. I have no idea what to do.

Chapter 16
Abuse

June 6th
Andy is so attentive and continues to phone me every day. He has asked me to go away with him for the weekend and, at first, I panicked, fearing that he might want sex. It will be the first time I have seen him in a while. He assures me there are no strings attached and we can take things very slowly. I am quite looking forward to the trip; it will be nice to get away from the flat, the dogs and the child for the weekend. *I wonder what he has in mind. Perhaps a nice bed and breakfast, somewhere by the sea. He has asked me to bring my passport for I D purposes, but I am hardly a teenager and wonder if we might be going abroad – woohoo!*

I have told Charlie I am going to Kent with Pandora and she is happy to cover for me. She often did the same when I stayed with Jude, albeit begrudgingly. This time she has been nothing but supportive and has even bought me a new bag.

Now I should start thinking about what to pack.

June 7th
I am ready for the off and surprised at how excited I am. I have hardly thought about Jude these past few days – well maybe a bit, but not in same way as before. My throat is still slightly tender and sometimes provokes the odd flashback which is thankfully negative. I have very few sweet memories now.

June 10th
Our weekend was the most wonderful surprise of my entire life. No man has ever gone to such trouble for me and it makes my soul wobble. Andy has the biggest heart in the whole universe and cannot be surpassed when it comes to chivalry. Now I am confident that the love will come.

He picked me up at midday when Charlie was at school and put my luggage in the boot of his car. He opened the passenger door like a true gentleman. He smiled a cheeky smile like an excited child as I jumped onto the seat in my usual, unladylike fashion – good job I rarely wear a skirt.

"Where are we going?"

"Bit nosey aint ya? Just wait and see."

We talked rubbish for a while and every so often, Andy burst into laughter for no apparent reason. I sensed he was terribly delighted about something – he was almost hysterical and I found that cute.

After an hour I noticed we were headed for Gatwick airport, but said nothing. The prospect of travelling abroad was thrilling, though I remained silent in case we were only going to Brighton.

We eventually pulled into the large car park at Gatwick which cost an arm and a leg for the weekend. Money is clearly no object to Andy, though I always notice things like that, being the skinflint that I am.

"Come on, Andy. I'm sick of the suspense, where are you taking me?"

He started to laugh again and then said, "Paris."

***

We stayed in a beautiful hotel right in the centre of Paris called Adagio which must have cost the earth. The food was magnificent and we spent each evening getting tipsy. During the day we wandered around, visiting many of the famous landmarks. I loved the Louvre, the Eiffel Tower, Notre Dame and best of all The Pantheon.

***

We had twin beds in our room and Andy remained on his best behaviour until the last night. It was yesterday – Sunday night, so we had begun to wind down and pack our things for the flight this morning.

"I've had such a good time, Andy, thank you. I don't deserve all this, but I'm going be completely honest with you from now on."

He smiled.

I had just settled down and was about to drift to sleep.

Andy came over to me and whispered, "Can I have a cuddle? Just a cuddle."

"Okay."

I felt his comforting arms around me and his warm body close to mine. The weekend had ignited a special bond between us. It was, and still is, my mission to fall in love with him. I turned around, held him tight and kissed him. It was a real kiss that lingered and felt right this time.

"You seem different, Eloise."

"I *feel* different – and I want to be with you."

To say, 'I love you' would have been a half truth, so I chose my words carefully. I decided to initiate the sex for once and wrapped my fingers around his erect penis. We continued to kiss slowly and passionately until our chins were covered in dribble. It was a warm night and soon our bodies were aglow with droplets as we writhed and made love like I have only seen in movies.

This was different. This was special, noble and honest – until I had my first ever 'Andy orgasm' and shouted, "Jude!"

Andy quickly withdrew and moved to his own bed. I watched as he sat, staring at the ceiling and a single tear fell onto his beautiful naked chest.

"I'm sorry, Andy. It's only force of habit. I haven't thought of Jude at all this weekend, honestly!"

I was telling the truth and have no idea why I shouted such a thing.

"Well at least you were in the room this time," he said, sarcastically.

"That's exactly it though. Didn't you feel how different it was? I was with you, not that lunatic. No more lies, remember?

"Okay. We'd best get some sleep. Early start in the morning."

I hardly slept at all. I worried that he had gone off me.

***

As we flew back to London, Andy was very quiet. He seemed much chirpier as we drove home in the car.

"I'm sorry I had a moody last night, I was feeling hurt."

"I know. I promise I'll never mention Jude again. He's out of my life now and I actually hate him."

"Good."

* * *

As I arrived home this morning, I realised one of my dogs, Gino was missing. I presumed he was with Frank. I was unpacking my things when there was loud knock at the door. It was Frank and he had a look of fury in his piggy eyes.

"I took Charlie to school this morning. It's his last exam and I'm picking him up at three."

"Don't you want me to fetch him?"

"No, he's staying with me."

"Come on, Frank, what's your problem? He never stays with you."

"He can't face his slag of a mother today, that's why. You haven't even noticed Gino is missing, have you?"

"I thought he was with you."

"No he's dead, had a massive seizure, not that you'd give a shit."

"Of course I give a shit," I answered, as tears streamed from my eyes and nose, right into my mouth. I was heartbroken.

"Well while you've been gallivanting God knows where, your son has lost his fucking dog and your fucking phone is always fucking switched off."

"We had terrible trouble with our phone signals in Kent."

"Kent, my arse" I drove past Pandora's twice and saw her in her front room. You were with that fucking Jude weren't you?"

"No, I wasn't, and who do you think you are, spying on me anyway?"

"You're stupid and need someone to look out for you."

"No, you're just jealous and WHY CAN'T I HAVE A BOYFRIEND ANYWAY? IT'S NONE OF YOUR FUCKING BUSINESS EVEN IF I DID."

I screamed so loud that I strained my bad throat. My voice went completely so I could no longer answer back. Frank pushed his way into my lounge and snatched my phone from the coffee table. Jude's number had been long gone so he found nothing, not even a telling text of any kind. He crashed the phone back down again. Andy's number is in my directory, and searching through it never occurred to Frank. There is little logic in that meat-head of his and Jude had provided a useful red-herring.

Frank walked toward me and put his face up to mine. "You should stay at home and look after our kid, you useless bitch. When I find out who you're fucking, he'll have some of this too." Then he punched me full on the nose, turned around and walked back out of the flat.

There was so much blood and the pain pierced through my skull.

Andy wants to see me one night this week and I will have to put him off. If he sees my face he will try to find Frank and give him a hiding. I will say I have the flu. My voice is funny so he will probably believe me. I have promised no more lies but I need to keep him out of all this shit.

June 12th

Andy is not best pleased with my excuse. He thinks I am avoiding him, and still worries about my feelings for Jude. I have assured him that Jude is in the past and promised to see him next week. Hopefully the bruising will have gone down enough to hide with foundation. I am still writing as much as I can manage each day. It keeps me sane in a strange way.

June 15th

The last couple of days have been pure misery. Andy has only called once and his conversation was stilted and half-hearted. I think I might be losing him.

Charlie is back and is very upset about the dog. It is sad although we still have the other one. I only hope his last A level exam went well in spite of his grief. He is being rather nice to me which is odd.

"How is your father?"

"Alright. I told him he shouldn't have hit you."

"Thanks."

"Who were you really with, Mum?"

"A nice man that I met recently. He took me to Paris."

Charlie's face dropped.

"I know you've split up with Dad, but you with a new bloke is too weird."

"I understand how you feel."

"It's horrible. What's his name?"

"Don't you think I deserve some happiness though, Charlie?" I asked, quickly changing the subject.

"I suppose so."

"And I made a good choice this time. He was a lovely fellla."

"Was?"

"Yes, was. It's over now so you don't have to worry. I didn't want him to see the bruises so cancelled our date and he went all huffy."

"Well he couldn't have been that great then."

"Oh he was, but all this pussyfooting around your dad and lying has worn me out and he can sense it. It's not his fault."

"Oh."

"Anyway, I'm gonna be single from now on, so stop worrying."

I knew he would go running to his father with his newly gleaned information and I hardly cared anymore. Then came the phone call.

"So another one has dumped ya then! Mr. No name! When will you ever learn, you stupid cow?"

"I am better off on my own, but I don't need you to tell me thank you, you fucking monstrosity!"

"You're getting old and haggard, and soon no one will want you anyway, you daft bitch!"

"Fuck off!"

***

June 21st

I have just returned from the hospital after a few days of confinement in the psychiatric ward. I had felt so alone after Frank screamed insults at me down the phone. The getting old part got to me the most. I had wasted my life on useless men and had little to show for it. I went into the kitchen and took handfuls of paracetamol. I cannot recall exactly how many. The doctor has given me a new type of antidepressant and sent me on my way; convinced I am no longer suicidal. I had only just finished my course of counselling sessions when all this happened and now I doomed to more. I *wanted* to die and still feel a sensation of confusion and nothingness. Why do they bother saving people like me who really want to exit their crap lives? They always think it is a cry for help or attention seeking. I have messed up my life to such an extent that it means nothing now. Neither to me nor anyone else. Psychiatrists really are shit. There has been no word from Andy either so he is probably history now.

***

Charlie had come home and found me unconscious on the sofa. I had enjoyed my long sleep and was disappointed to be woken by a nurse. She told me that Frank and Charlie were at the hospital until I was out of the woods. Pandora was totally unaware at first, and I saw no one for three days. I had a panic attack on the third night that was so bad I needed sedation. I must have slept for hours and as I opened my eyes I saw a beautiful face. The face that belonged to Jude...

He kissed me softly on the cheek and whispered, "I love you."

"I love you too," I whispered back.

I closed my eyes briefly, and when I opened them again he was gone.

I sat bolt upright. "Nurse, quickly, come here."

"What is it, my love?"

"Was there a tall dark man here a few moments ago, or was I dreaming?"

"Yes, he was here, but it was a few hours ago and we couldn't wake you up properly."

I found my trousers in the bedside cabinet and checked the pocket. My phone was still there with a message from Pandora.

'That bastard Frank came to my house and told me you'd taken an overdose. I hope you are okay. I couldn't get to see you because I've been ill and full of germs. Jude messaged me on Facebook and asked how you were. I thought he'd heard about your overdose, so

I told him they'd pumped the pills out. But he didn't know, and now I've put my foot in it. Please stay away from him if he gets in touch. See you as soon as I can. P X'

It *was* him and he was the only one who bothered to come and see me.

June 27th

I am forcibly keeping myself busy and slowly recovering with the help of antidepressants and bloody boring counselling. Still no word from Andy and my life is rather dull. Pandora has visited me a couple of times and her advice remains like a rock in my mind. Much as I yearn to, I have made no attempt to contact Jude.

Chapter 17
Getting old

July 1st

In just under a fortnight I will be forty-five years old – how depressing! And what do I have to show for those forty-five years? I have achieved very little when I think about it. I have had a string of disastrous relationships, few friends and a son who finds me disappointing – and that is putting it politely. I fear that Andy is long gone – and just when I was beginning to like him. I am such an idiot! Anyway, I shall plod on and continue to exist in my dream-like world of writing. I can be who I want, do what I like and make good things happen in my make-believe world. No one can hurt me and no one can take what is inside my mind. My novels have been self-indulgent thus far, and largely based on my crap life. The next book will be something uplifting and completely fictitious – this could definitely improve my disposition. Maybe I could write something funny or perhaps I can create the perfect love story – and find the man I have always dreamed of.

I have thought about Jude, since I saw his face in my semi-conscious state. I wonder if somewhere in his sick mind there are genuine feelings of love and empathy; feelings that are buried so deep, they are twisted and lost. I have read there is little hope and no cure for sociopaths although I sometimes find myself in denial. I am sure he loved me. Why else did he visit me in hospital without making a fuss? He must have been worried and he must have cared what was happening to me. For over a year he has caused me much sorrow and pain. But there were those times when he made me feel I could fly. He took away my fears and no one could ever touch me like that again. I was once an angel and now I am resigned to a life without love or comfort. There is no one to run to now, so I must learn to run to me and like myself again. I am glad I sent him that letter. It was composed and bereft of anger. I hope he realised that I will always care about him. There has been no reply, although that was not my intent and is probably for the best.

July 3rd

Today I received a letter from Andy. It was lovely to receive a real letter for a change. Emails and texts are so impersonal and only bills seem to pop through the letterbox nowadays. I was afraid to open it at first, fearing it was a Dear John like the one I sent Jude.

'Dear Ellie,

I'm so sorry I've not been in touch. You hurt me and made me feel second best to Jude. I thought I deserved more than that to be honest. I will always love you and be here for you if you ever need me. If you manage to get that madman out of your head, then I will still be here. I won't contact you again unless you ask me to and leave the decision entirely in your hands.

I hope you are well and happy. Have a great birthday.

Love Andy xxxx'

It made me cry and he even remembered my birthday. Just as I had resigned myself to the life of a singleton, my world is once again jogged out of kilter. I will have to take my time and think this through for at least a couple of weeks. He will probably meet someone else and I will only have myself to blame. Oh God.

July 7th

Bloody hell, another letter has arrived and this one is from Jude. We have all gone mad and sent the bloody post office into meltdown. How very old-fashioned! Soon we will be using quills and wax seals. I had not expected this at all! I wish it were genuine but my cynicism tells me there is more chance of pissing in the Pope's hat. It is only another game and a new tact – you can bet your life.

'Dear Cathy, (yawn)

I hope you're better. I came to see you at the hospital and you were away with the fairies, but they said that you'd be alright. I've missed you and I'm sorry for what happened. I stopped taking my tablets because I hate drugs. You know I was addicted to them once. My doctor has promised me that my new meds are different to anything I took when I was a kid. So I'm taking them again like a good boy and my mood is much better.

The doctor also tells me I have Post-Traumatic Stress Disorder. This throws a completely new light on things. The therapist is talking about regression to finally get to the bottom of things and hopefully out of my system forever.

It's your birthday soon and I've got you a present. Can we have lunch one day so I can give it to you? I promise not to be pushy or anything.
Love Heathcliff
Xxxxxxxxxxx'

How can I trust him after all that has happened? I have done a bit of online research since reading his letter and he does fit the criteria. A doctor even wrote a paper on how some people with PTSD are misdiagnosed with sociopathic disorders. People posting on the *I survived a sociopath* forums poo pooed the idea but it certainly held my interest for a while.

* * *

I have just sent Jude an email. Yes, I am back in the 21st century with my heart desperately searching for my sleeve again. What am I like? I simply said it was nice to hear from him and all that rubbish. It has been hardly two hours since I received his letter and I am acting like an eager drip already.

* * *

Today is Charlie's 18th birthday and I gave him a card and one hundred pounds. Frank is taking him out to dinner this evening and obviously I am not invited. It makes no odds to me. They can choke on it for all I care.

July 8th

It will take a few days to get my head together, so I have arranged to see Jude on my birthday and he is over the moon.

Frank and Charlie practically ignore me now, so I can do what I like. We are meeting at the steak house again. Since my crash in the car park, I always make sure I am five minutes late. Jude is a stickler for time-keeping so is usually at the table as I park. It still freaks me out and I look like the worst driver on the planet, tentatively pulling in. I remind myself of an overly cautious snail. It would embarrass me if Jude was watching. He is a terrible piss-taker. I still worry that I could be charged for the broken fence or even prosecuted for leaving the scene. There are cameras everywhere, but seemingly they were turned off that day. Perhaps they are simply a deterrent.

July 9th

My nerves are hanging out of my ears. I have no appetite and it is impossible to write. So much for my hilarious comedy romance! Every time I write so much as a line, I delete it because it is shit. The second book is still open ended.

Pandora made one of her not so regular visits earlier today. Charlie skulks around the house much of the time since finishing sixth form but, thankfully, this morning he was out so I could lie to my heart's content.

"What are you doing for your birthday?"

"Charlie's taking me out to dinner."

"Aww, that's sweet, he's a good boy sometimes."

"Yeah, he is sometimes."

"Aren't you seeing Andy?"

"No, we've split up."

"Oh no, are you okay?"

"Yeah, fine. I've such bad luck with men."

"Oh, who needs them anyway? We should start going out more again. Shall we do a pub lunch next Sunday? I'll treat you."

"Yeah, that'll be lovely. We should go to The Bugle, there's all day music."

***

It has been a long time since we last went out together. We used to have so much fun eating and dancing, I do so miss it.

July 10th

Only two more days and it will be my birthday. Jude sends me a little message at least once a day, whilst keeping his promise not to be ambitious. In the beginning we had planned to be together when the time was right. This would have been nearing the perfect time with Charlie off to university soon. But things turned ugly at many turns and blew us off target. We are defeated by whatever has damaged us. As a child, I imagined tragedy in love was reserved for stories and books that old people fuss about. They were usually about death too and, of course, Jude and I are very much alive. I thought that I would grow up, get married and have lots of happy children running amok. I pictured a handsome husband who kissed me every night as he returned from work. We would sit by the fire and talk, while the children were tucked up in their fluffy beds. There was no hurt or suffering in my dream. There were no beatings, shouting or manipulations. I would love and be loved. My life with Frank was a very different tale. Last year it seemed I had a second chance to live my dream with a like-minded soul. A man who welcomed a simple life and the joy that is born from its tranquillity – the idea turned me giddy. I even toyed with the notion of another baby but I am too old now. Jude has never had a child and I wonder if one could have saved him. In reality he could have been a terrible father – even a dangerous one. We will likely continue our peculiar friendship way into our dotage, still squabbling as we walk along a seaside promenade and then laughing 'til we cry. We will never have a healthy relationship as lovers– I know that now. Such a shame!

July 11th

Frank really is unbelievable. He had the audacity to phone, inviting me for a meal tomorrow night for my birthday. *As if*! He asked the same thing a while back, soon after we had separated. He said we could go out as friends so I thought, *why not?* By the end of the evening, he was drunk and trying to get his leg over. Evidently his luck with women has not fared too well recently which is hardly surprising – given he is a ghastly sod!

"No thanks," was my flat answer.

"What you doin' then?"

"Lunch with Pandora and then a night with the telly, if you must know."

"That doesn't sound very exciting."

"Go away."

I have given up caring what he and Charlie think of me. Even if they followed me tomorrow it would make no difference. I would probably pick up something heavy and smash it over Frank's head for starters. I would love to see their faces. I am sure they will find out one day. Jude may have turned my world into disarray but at least I have felt things in that muddled world. Things I would never have known without him.

July 12th

Charlie wished me happy birthday this morning and gave me some flowers and a card. He even kissed me on my head.

"I'm off out with Luke, Mum. Have a nice day."

"Thanks, Charlie; you too."

Pandora dropped by again a bit later– the second time this week! She wants our friendship back to how it was and so do I. We have a lot of catching up to do and I will tell her the truth about everything on Sunday.

"Happy Birthday! Here's a little present."

It was a beautiful necklace.

"That's so sweet, I love it, thank you."

We had a couple of coffees and then she got up to leave.

"Have a lovely day, Eloise and I'll see you at 2 o'clock on Sunday."

"Goodbye, Pandora."

"Goodbye? You're only going out for lunch, not joining the Foreign Legion." She was still laughing as she shut the door behind her.

My new necklace is beautiful, but will stay in its box for now. It would be awkward if Jude's gift turns out to be something similar. He would hate Pandora for getting in first. I want to avoid confrontation at all costs. It is my birthday after all, and although birthdays are becoming less appealing as I get older – I need to have a good one today. I had better leave soon. Nothing has changed after all that has happened. I continue to put Jude before everyone else – even myself. If only I could let go. I know this is wrong and I know I am doomed.

***

Pandora

This was the last entry to the journal of Eloise Fry. She had disappeared. Something was wrong on the morning of her birthday. There was a feeling of sadness and her eyes were as dead as Jude's. She still had her smile but something was missing. Her farewell was strange and made me anxious for a while. I cast my doubts aside, hoping they were fanciful and went on with my day. There was a time when she could never have fooled me, but the last time I saw her she almost had. She had learned to hide behind a façade and was very good at it. Now it was my job to find her.

Chapter 18
The Search

Pandora

As I waited for Eloise in the pub that Sunday, I had a strange feeling in the well of my stomach. She was very late. I sat at the table and repeatedly dialled her number. There was no reply. After an hour, I gave up and went home.

I thought perhaps she was unwell and made myself some lunch, forcing my mind to underplay the situation.

That same evening there was a knock at my door. It was Frank.

"Is Eloise with you?"

He looked more angry than truly worried.

"No, I haven't seen her."

"Charlie said you had lunch on her birthday and she hasn't been seen since."

She had lied to me and said she was lunching with Charlie. I wondered if perhaps she had met Andy again although my instincts told me otherwise – surely she would have mentioned it. Frank's gait was menacing and I needed to be liberal with my answers.

"Yes, we had lunch and I wanted her to watch a band with me today, but she didn't get back to me."

Now I was worried so thought it best to be honest about having no contact since Friday. She was obviously not with me anyway – he could see that.

"Where the fuck is she? She's not answering her phone. I'll have to report her missing."

"Perhaps you should."

"Her clothes, make-up and even her precious laptop are still at the flat. I'm ringing the police."

As he stomped away, a foreboding ambushed my whole body. She had been missing for three days and taken none of her possessions. It was unsafe to play dumb with Frank now. That could place her in more danger and we needed to find her, although I honestly knew nothing.

Then it occurred to me that she could have been with Jude. *How did that ever get past me*? I thought back to how evasive she had been of late, so it would make perfect sense. If my hunch was correct, I hoped they had just run off together – they both loved a bit of drama. I would have to find a way of contacting him and warn them that Frank was on the warpath.

***

After searching online I found Jude's author webpage and his mobile number was listed under contact. Then, with shaking hands, I dialled it.

"Hello."

"Hi Jude, it's Pandora."

"Hello, Pandora; what's up?"

"Have you seen Eloise at all?"

"No, not for a while. She phoned me just before her birthday, why do you ask and how have you got my number?"

"I found it on the internet. She's gone missing. No one's seen her since Friday, so I just wondered if you'd heard anything."

"God, I feel terrible now. She asked to meet me and I said no."

"Why?"

"All we ever do is argue so I put her off. She sounded depressed and was going on about funerals; she even told me what hymns she wanted."

"Jerusalem?"

"Yes and Christina Aguilera, and something about a will hidden in her drawer. I thought it was just emotional blackmail. What have I done, Pandora? If she's in trouble it'll be my fault."

"Not necessarily, Jude. Don't worry; I'm going to find her."

"Have you tried phoning?"

"Yes, but she's not answering. She's probably run out of battery now anyway.

"Let me know as soon as you hear anything."

"Will do. Bye."

My initial inclination was to believe him, because that is exactly what she would have said. Then I began to feel unsettled and wondered if he had anything to hide. He was gracious and his concern was convincing although something felt wrong. He had caused her so much misery and I had always frowned upon their abnormal relationship. So why should I trust him now? I had to find a way to the truth but had no concept of how. The worry and fear left me unable to sleep. I imagined all kinds of terrible things and could do nothing. There were no clues anywhere. As I busted my brain to find a solution, I remembered the key Eloise had given me. I was certain that Charlie would be staying with Frank so decided to rescue her diaries the following morning.

* * *

The dairies were now safely in my care along with the draft of her second novel. I opened the first one, and then there was a knock at the door. It was Frank again. This time he looked lost and tearful so I invited him to sit down.

"They've found a woman's body, Pandora."

"Oh my God, surely it's not Eloise."

"They said she's small and blonde."

"But lots of women are small and blonde. It doesn't necessarily mean it's her."

"The body was in a car though – her car."

He looked to the floor and tears fell onto his lap. It appeared that he did feel something for her after all. If he had treated her better however, none of this would have happened but I kept that thought to myself. I was shocked and unable to cry although knew it would come later and probably go on for days.

"I need to identify her," he said, trying to pull himself together. "Will you come with me?"

The prospect of seeing my best friend on a mortuary slab was unthinkable. I went along however, thinking it was the right thing to do.

* * *

They say that people appear peaceful when they die – all waxen and free from pain. Eloise was not like that at all. She was bloated with prominent veins on her temple, looking almost agonised.

Her car was found in a secluded copse in Epping Forrest the day after her disappearance and we wondered why she had chosen to die there. There was an almost finished litre of vodka on her lap, along with an empty bottle of tablets. The labels had been removed from the pills so further tests would be needed. There would also be a post mortem. Apparently there was little to identify her apart from the registration number. I wondered where her bag had gone. She never went anywhere without her bag. There was a suicide note in the glove box which was verified because of her unique untidy handwriting.

'My life is a mess and I have decided to leave it behind. I hope there is somewhere to go from here – somewhere without pain and complication. I doubt very much that I will be missed. All that I leave are my personal possessions and each of you can take your pick. I had a small insurance policy which will likely be void now. It can be found in my knickers drawer. So Frank, you will probably have to pay for the funeral. Put me in a fucking skip if you so wish.
Bye
Eloise'

The certificate declared suicide as the cause of her death. The pills were identified as antidepressants. She had been prescribed them although I wondered why the label had been removed. The funeral was scheduled for Monday July 22nd and Frank took charge of the proceedings. It would have been imprudent for me to interfere. Eloise had a rather morbid side to her character and often talked of her own funeral, even when we were young. Did it really matter anyway? She was gone and I had no belief in the afterlife – but still felt overwhelmed with guilt. I found Andy's number amongst her papers and called him with the sad news. He was inconsolable. He asked me where the funeral would take place because he wanted to be there. I warned him to steer clear of Frank and he agreed to discretion, saying he wanted no trouble.

I would have to wait a week before I saw my friend laid to rest. Meanwhile I began to read her diaries. Much of her story made me smile at first, until it became darker by the page. It felt perverse in a way, reading her private thoughts although she had given me the key and wanted me to have them.

As I read on, I was astonished and disappointed in equal quantity. Her lies and acting had been outstanding. The last few months of her life must have been intolerable and I had been left totally unaware. I wish she had sought help and comfort from me and I wish I could have stopped her. I finally reached the last entry. It was then my suspicions about Jude were confirmed.

***

It took me just two days and two nights to finish the Journals. In five days it would be her funeral and her revelations would need to remain secret for now. It was not fitting to bring her dark and furtive practices to light just yet. It would remain between me and Eloise until I found out what part Jude had played in this. I needed a well thought out, devious plan. I decided to make initial contact by phoning him with the news of Eloise's death – she was, as he used to maintain, 'the love of his life' after all.

"Nooooooooo," he groaned, as though his heart had been ripped from his chest.

"I'm so sorry I had to tell you over the phone, Jude, but you needed to know."

The noise radiating from my mobile was demented. There were no words, only howling that would cease very briefly, giving pause for whimpering sobs, and then came the howling again. I found his reaction rather over-baked. Most people are quiet at first after shocking news but Jude went berserk immediately. I thought it would take at least a moment to register. Obviously people respond differently to sudden grief, though I have never heard anything quite like Jude's performance. He had put any banshee and even the Mexican wailing ghost to shame. It was relentless so I hung up on him in the end. He called me back about an hour later, asking about the funeral details. He was calmer by then, though still weeping as he spoke. He said he should keep away to avoid confrontation and would take some flowers the day after. He wanted his moment with 'Cathy' to be private.

He was a player but a stupid one by all accounts. I could play like the best of them and easily win. Jude had trouble playing guitar so this would be easy. I was detached from him emotionally after a fashion, so would walk it and have his fucking head on a stick as a trophy.

Chapter 19
Wake

It was a difficult to celebrate a life that had been wilfully taken. There were no eulogies during the service – I can only imagine it was too difficult for her family. What could they say to befit a death by suicide? In the cemetery there were some muffled mumblings and a few tears – which were barely heard as they interwove with a light squealing wind. It was a shadowy noise that seemed to whisper her name over and over.

A picture of Eloise was placed in the middle of the buffet just like a centrepiece. I smiled to myself, imagining what she would have made of it. She would have definitely found it amusing. My fond memories of the laughter we had always shared held me together that day. I tried hard not to snigger – heaven forbid I should disparage this sombre pantomime – Eloise would have guffawed.

The atmosphere was awkward without so much as a quirky anecdote – yet there were plenty of those to be had. Her relatives talked quietly as they drowned their sorrow in booze. Frank and Charlie mingled and hardly said a word to me. They always saw me as some terrible influence so her death was probably my fault in their ignorant minds. The absence of Jude and Andy was the most extraordinary thing of all. They had been such a paramount part of her world in recent months. This was the celebration of a life that very few were aware of. It was a farce and a lie.

After a while I managed to gracefully escape unnoticed. As soon as I returned home, I phoned Andy. I had envisaged him as a good, no-nonsense man and potential invaluable ally.

"Hello, Andy. I'm Eloise's friend, was that you at the funeral?"

"Yes, I saw you, I guessed you were Pandora."

"Listen, Andy, I need to talk to you but we'll have to meet up, I can't do it over the phone."

"Okay, but what's going on?"

"I'm not sure her death was suicide."

"What?"

"I think maybe someone else was involved and need some help."

"Are you sure?"

"Yes."

"Her ex-husband?"

"No, not him."

"Not that fucking Jude!"

"I think so."

I was surprised and relieved he knew something of Jude – at least there would be less explaining to do now.

"Okay, where shall we meet?"

"Perhaps you should come to my house."

"Alright. Give me your address and I'll come tonight."

Andy deserved to know the truth as much as I did. He had loved her and I saw just how much as he stood clutching that rose.

Andy arrived at my house within two hours. From the moment I saw him; a million butterflies fluttered, not only through my stomach, but my entire body. *Was it simply nerves?* I wondered. He was a vision and so much more than Jude in every way. His eyes and were kind and his smile sincere. Feelings of awkwardness and guilt quickly averted my eyes from his. *Had there been some kind of instant attraction?* This was neither the time nor the place. After a stumbling exchange of greetings, I invited him to sit down.

"Would you like a coffee?"

"Yes please."

As I waited for the kettle to boil, I wondered what on earth I was doing.

***

"So what's being going on, Pandora?"

"Eloise left me these."

I handed him the opened diary.

"This was the last thing she ever wrote."

"How many are there?"

"Lots, but this is the important one."

I could see his tears forming as he read.

"She was seeing that bastard again!"

"Yes. I didn't want to hurt you, Andy but you deserve to know."

"I wish I didn't."

"I know it's hard, but when I saw you today, I could see how much you loved her."

"She didn't love me back though, did she?"

"I think she did though, Andy, that's the thing and she probably didn't even know it. She would've given her right arm for someone like you a couple of years ago – don't forget, I know her better than anyone."

"Except for him," he said, looking down to his lap.

"But that was all fantasy. He used her and made her his victim. It wasn't love; even she knew that deep down. It's all in the diaries."

"Can I read the rest of it?"

"I don't think that's such a good idea. I'll tell you all you need to know."

"Okay but why haven't you told the police?

"It just says she was on her way to see him and they'll want proof that she did."

We had to find a way to get to Jude, learn the truth and expose him somehow. He would simply manipulate the police, saying he had cancelled their date or some such tedious yarn. We needed to know what happened that day and make a plan to find out.

***

I poured myself a large glass of wine and Andy another coffee. We sat and made small talk, getting nowhere fast and I wondered if this had been a good idea.

"I could really do with a drink," he said.

"It's a shame you're driving."

"Is there a guest house nearby?"

I could tell he was hinting to stay and he really needed some alcohol. I felt responsible for his anguish so made him an offer.

"Have you got work tomorrow?"

"I've got my own business, so I don't need to go in."

"You can stay in my spare room if you like."

"Actually that might be an idea."

"We can sort this out sooner if you stick around. Nice glass of wine then?"

"Yeah, go for it."

After a few drinks Andy appeared more relaxed. I told him stories from the past, and we laughed at the anecdotes which were cruelly overlooked at the funeral. Andy said he would like to throttle a confession from Jude. I told him we had to be meticulous and stressed the importance of calm. We thought it best to confront Jude face to face, but needed good reason to visit. We decided I could phone first, offering him pictures and keepsakes of Eloise. Of course I would need to ask for his address. If he knew it was found with the papers from her desk it could make him suspicious. I was certain he knew nothing of her journals however, which was a Godsend. The idea was perfect in the fog of our drunken minds. I would introduce Andy as my boyfriend and we would express concern and offer comfort for his terrible loss. He would be absorbed by the attention and his melodramatic ramblings were a certainty. Of course he would be oblivious to everyone else's mourning and *genuine* grief.

After several more drinks, I offered Andy another. As he took it, he kept hold of my hand. His eyes were alluring and told me just one thing – my instincts knew exactly what that was.

"You're so like her."

His words angered me a little. Eloise had only been buried that morning and he was looking for comfort from her best friend. I was angry for her and sad for me – he wanted a replacement. I quickly turned back to the subject of Jude.

"I'll ring Jude tomorrow."

"Okay', I'd better get some sleep now if you don't mind."

"No you go up. Bathroom's straight ahead and spare room's second on the right. I think there's a spare toothbrush in the cabinet."

"I really appreciate this, Pandora."

"No problem. Night!"

***

I sat and deliberated long into the night and was almost sober by dawn. Confronting Jude would need an iron will and a special power of reserve. I was uneasy about Andy's involvement now and wished I had never made that call. He was different from what I had expected. Would he be up to such a challenging task? I was disappointed with the way he had looked at me and wondered if he was just another player. He seemed so sad at the cemetery that morning, even before he had spotted me. Surely it must have been genuine. I thought maybe Jude had made me suspicious of all men and I was losing my grip on reality. Perhaps Andy had drunkenly transferred his feelings for Eloise onto me. Once or twice I noticed his eyes close as I talked. *Did he fantasise he was listening to her*? I had felt isolated, desperately needing someone to lean on and someone to listen. It was a mistake. Andy was solid and reliable but now I feared taking him along could be a waste of time. What if we discovered nothing? Jude would hardly admit to a crime without evidence especially in front of a man. I was numb and angry which made me quite fearless. Andy was different. His feelings were too raw and transparent. In a strange way I was attracted to him even though he was rather wet behind the ears – perhaps because of it. As I sat alone, arriving back to reality, I decided that Andy would be nothing more than a liability. Jude was a dangerous man. I had always known that, but had never realised the magnitude of his lunacy. Now it was indisputable because of his lies and all that Eloise had written – I knew him as she did. I had to prove that they met on her on her Birthday – I was sure of it. Our plan was lame and full of holes – a farce built on drunken ramblings Andy was inexperienced in treachery and games. I had to do this on my own. But how would I remove Andy from the equation? After mulling the situation over and over, I decided upon a new strategy. I knew it was a dangerous idea but the only one that could possibly work. It was time to stop pussyfooting around.

***

The next morning, I awoke early and made some tea and toast. Andy was still quiet so I thought it best to wake him. I needed to get him out of the house.

I knocked on the door and he answered. "Come in."

He looked so handsome, not at all dishevelled and I wondered if he had actually slept. He thanked me and began to drink his tea.

"Sit down, Pandora," he demanded softly.

There was an uncomfortable silence as he continued to drink. "I'll go downstairs and finish my breakfast."

"No wait."

He began to weep like a girl.

"What is it?"

"Will you hold me?"

I was sorry for him so climbed into bed and lay by his side. He was broken and although it felt wrong, I complied and hugged him. He was wearing boxer shorts thankfully and there was no evidence of broom-handle syndrome. We held each other closely and then he kissed me. There was no overwhelming passion in the act but it was warm and comforting for us both. We had a strong connection through Eloise and I wondered if that was all it was. Andy was nothing like the men I was used to. My choice in men had invariably been as ridiculous as my best friend's – well almost. Neither of us were well rested and so we became each other's consolation as we fell into a deep sleep.

We slept until noon and I quickly went downstairs whilst Andy got washed and dressed. I had taken breakfast to his room deliberately and luckily there were no sexual demands. I would have gladly gone through with it however, had there been – I needed to gain his trust. As he entered the living room, I regaled my well-practiced lie.

"I just rang Jude."

"What did he say?"

"He's away somewhere and won't be back for a week."

"Does he want some of Ellie's things?"

"Well he couldn't really say no could he?"

"He's fallen for it then. Good," he said, looking smug. "So we'll go as soon as he gets back."

"Yeah, I'll let you know as soon as he rings me."

"Can I see you before that?"

"I think we both need some time, Andy. Let's wait 'til after we see Jude."

"Okay, well I'd better go now."

He had believed every word and I felt like a fraud. He kissed my cheek at the door and then walked to his car. I had no idea if I would ever see him again.

Chapter 20
The sting

Adrenalin raced through my entire body as I drove to Jude's house the following afternoon. I repeatedly checked my bag, making sure that my mace spray and phone were still there. I knew he would be home because of his ridiculous timetable.

"Pandora!"

"You recognise me then?"

"Yes, vaguely from the 80's, and from pictures on Facebook."

"What happened to Cathy?" I asked sarcastically.

My coolness was a sham. I was terrified and needed to play this to perfection.

"I didn't realise you knew I called her that."

"I know everything, I was her best friend."

I could hear the dogs barking in the lounge.

"They think you're Cathy, you sound just like her."

He looked uneasy as he invited me in. His house was exactly as Eloise had described. The guitars, the artefacts, the dogs and the Wurlitzer were all there and I felt her presence, as though her soul was trapped in the walls.

"What do you want, Pandora and how do you know where I live?

"Your address was amongst her things."

"Oh I see. I thought I was just a secret she was ashamed of. I'm surprised she left stuff like that lying around. She never even told me where she lived."

He was acting sorry for himself. However, I knew his game now and played along.

"I've brought you some photos and poems, things you might like to have."

"Thank you, I'll treasure them."

A tear rolled down his cheek as he noticed the photo on the top of the pile. It was one that he had taken when they walked his dogs in the fields. He wiped it away, put the bundle down and walked towards his kitchen. His performance was superb. I hoped and wished that a little of it was real – she and her memory deserved that at least.

I followed him into the kitchen.

"Would you like some tea?" he asked.

"I'd rather have a coffee."

"I don't drink coffee. I used to keep some for Cathy, but threw it away after she died."

His face began to contort as though he was forcing back tears.

"This is so hard, it's only been a few days, forgive me."

"That's okay, Jude. Don't worry."

I desperately tried to stop my hand from shaking as I placed it on his shoulder. He turned around and smiled. He looked much older and very different to how I remembered. But that smile! It magically took away those twenty six years and his face suddenly illuminated.

"Do you remember when I came to see you in the eighties after you finished with Eloise?"

"I vaguely remember you from back then, but don't recall you coming to see me," he answered, looking more uncomfortable by the second. "Shall we go and sit in the lounge?"

"You don't remember then?" I persisted.

"I was high most of the time in those days, Pandora."

I suspected his puzzled expression was contrived so decided to suspend our awkward exchange for the time being. We spoke of Eloise and although he was a lunatic, I think he somehow loved her in the only way that he could. Jude had always been an enigma and attracted many women. He surged an energy that could never be bettered, especially to a vulnerable heart – or even one not so vulnerable. I had warned Eloise so many times to steer clear of the monster that was Jude. Half of me had feared what he might do and the other half felt envy. She had been on an emotional journey that was rarely pleasant but she had felt so alive.

We drank tea as Jude thumbed through photographs of Eloise one by one. The look on his face as he gazed at her *did* almost resemble love. At that moment all I felt was fear and an insane kind of jealousy.

He was obviously curious by my pained expression and said, "You've never liked me, have you, Pandora? Cathy gave me the impression you disapproved."

My heart was pumping so fast, I could hardly answer and just managed to say, "You couldn't be more wrong, Jude."

"What do you mean?"

"I often said you needed a break from each other because of the arguments, but I've never hated you, rather the contrary in fact. She was always known for stretching the truth a bit.

He looked utterly confused and luckily failed to notice my constant trembling.

"Are you sure you don't you remember the night I came to your flat?"

"I told you – my memory's not what it was, Pandora!"

Then I decided to help him recall what really happened that night back in 1986 – if he indeed had forgotten which I doubt.

***

My temper was raging as I headed toward Jude's flat. I had left Eloise at home in bed from where she refused to budge. He opened the door and was definitely on something but shocked to see me nonetheless.

"What do you want?"

"I'm furious with you, Jude. You've left Eloise in a terrible way and your behaviour's been disgusting!"

"She knew it wouldn't last. It was just a rebound thing. I was in love with Sharon all the time."

"You told her that was all over."'

"I thought it was. Then I realised I wanted her back. She's coming to live with me in a few days."

His words were cold and remorseless and I felt myself beginning to boil over. He just stood, staring at me with his empty dark eyes. I knew he was dangerous and unhinged but could hardly contain my anger any longer.

"You are a psychotic bastard."

He laughed.

"You've broken her heart, Jude and I'm left to pick up the pieces. You even tried to throttle her for nothing. She should never have gone back to you. I might even go to the police myself."

I stood as far from the door and his reach as I could, making sure to avoid an attempt of assault.

"Come here, Pandora."

"No, I'm perfectly alright here, thank you very much."

He stepped towards me and gently took my hand. "She wouldn't leave me alone, Pandora. I tried to end it several times but she wouldn't listen."

Eloise could be a tenacious little thing although I knew he was lying. He suddenly moved even closer and kissed my cheek. He looked at me and suddenly those familiar dead black eyes became filled with something I cannot begin to describe. I could see what Eloise saw, as though I *was* her. If this sudden sparkle, which he adopted so readily, was the thing that bound her to love him, then in that moment, I loved him too. He led me into his hall, up the stairs and into his bedroom. My dazed and dreamlike form made resistance impossible. I was frightened and ecstatic as I wondered what would happen next.

He gently cupped the back of my head and pulled my mouth towards his. I had nothing to compare his kiss to. It was beautiful – as though it was my first ever. I was greatly aroused, but repulsed at myself for experiencing such pleasure from a man whom I hated. Now I understood his power but knew he felt nothing – it was all just a sick game.

"Come to my bed, Pandora," he whispered.

We sat on the bed and he gave me a pill with some water. I obeyed without giving it a thought and soon I was hallucinating. Everything became colourful and vivid – it must have been acid. Even his dick looked like a real python. We had sex for hours which was erotic, passionate and never ending. Perhaps it was the drugs. I am unsure because I had never taken acid before that night and have never taken it since.

We stayed together the whole night and as soon as I came to my senses the next morning, I left. He was still asleep and I vowed never to see him again. I must have been mad. I could have caught something from him – I felt so ashamed and decided to try and forget.

***

Jude continued to claim he had no recollection of that night. I decided not to mention my hatred and repulsion because that would have ruined my plan. He was aware that he had bewitched me however which made for a very smug expression on his evil face.

"Did you really have feelings for me, Pandora?"

"Yes, I did."

"Then why didn't I ever see you again?"

"I felt so guilty. Eloise would have killed me, and besides you had a girlfriend."

"Oh that didn't last anyway."

"Well to be honest, now Eloise has gone, I thought we might … you know?"

"What do it?" he asked, looking surprised but flattered.

"If *you* want to."

"Why not? We could give it a try."

It was clear that he felt nothing and simply wanted another victim to massage his horrendous ego. However, he had played straight into my hands.

"I was always envious of you two," I confessed. She used to tell me about how romantic you were and there's been no romance in my life for years."

He moved from his armchair and sat next to me on the couch. He held my hand and in true Jude style, flicked that magic switch that ignited the fire in his eyes. It was important for my fear to remain hidden. My hand shook inside his and I blamed it on my strong feelings for him.

We kissed and I felt the same stirring as before which made my heart and stomach ache with guilt. I silently apologised to Eloise, when suddenly something warm filled my solar plexus – It was her giving me the green light to go.

I pulled away. "I hated Eloise at times, Jude."

"Why?"

"Because you loved her so much, yet she always whined and complained about you. She didn't deserve you. I know it's a dreadful thing to say, but I'm glad she's out of the way now."

"She could be a selfish cow, Pandora."

"I know. I hated it when she took the piss out of you. She used to say you couldn't write or play the guitar."

"I didn't know she had such a low opinion of me," he said and his sadness looked quite genuine.

"Don't be upset, Jude. I'll never treat you like that."

He smiled and then I stuck my tongue into his mouth so forcefully that he almost choked. He had to believe that I loved him. My mixed feelings for him had always been such that to pull this off would be easy. He was an enigma but had to be stopped. I needed to avenge Eloise's death. I fumbled around by his flies and felt his dick was stiff.

"Let's go to your bedroom."

"Okay."

We almost ran to his bedroom, tearing our clothes off as we went. We fell naked onto his bed and the rampant sex began. It felt so good, even without the drugs and he knew exactly what to do with that huge thing of his. We came simultaneously and the whole thing took less than ten minutes. We lay on his bed, drenched in sweat and satisfied.

"Do you think we just let Eloise down, Pandora?"

"No, I laughed, she's dead and buried."

"That's a bit harsh. You sounded so upset on the phone."

"I didn't want to come across as a total bitch, did I? But I'm glad I don't have to listen to her constant whinging anymore."

"She killed herself here, Pandora."

"So you did see her on her Birthday?" I said, trying to look shocked, although I was a little surprised by his sudden confession.

"Yes."

***

He told me they had met at the steak house for lunch and Eloise was in a jolly mood. He was considerably less chirpy, but had no intention of spoiling her day. He gave her a card with a book voucher apparently, which I imagine hardly blew her mind. After lunch they went back to his house and listened to some music. Eloise had complained she was always unhappy without Jude and wanted them to be together properly. He told her that it could never work because they fought too much. She began to shout and accuse him of cyber-whoring with women.

"No wonder you don't want me to live with you. I'd see exactly what you get up to."

He protested his innocence and just replied, "See what I mean?"

He had been feeling particularly low for a couple of days, wanting to throw in the towel. His books were not selling and his hip and back pain was getting worse. His doctors had told him he suffered from Post-Traumatic Stress disorder and offered him regression therapy. It had cheered him up at first, so he decided to arrange a birthday treat for Eloise. However, the thought of reliving childhood abuse terrified him and by the time they met, he was seriously depressed. He had accumulated many tablets over the weeks, as he often refused to take them. He had also bought a huge bottle of vodka days before as he contemplated suicide. Eventually he confided this to Eloise and told her it was the wrong time for them to get closer.

"Oh it'll never be the right fucking time, will it?" she complained.

"No, I don't think it ever will."

By this time she was crying and Jude put his arms around her as his own tears began to flow. They realised that no matter how much they loved each other, they could never be happy together or anywhere else. They decided they would be better off dead. That was when Eloise talked of funerals, hymns and the little she would leave behind. They scribbled notes together and Jude stated the money from his house should be donated to a dog rescue centre.

They made love in his bedroom for the last time and then opened the vodka. Jude said that Eloise drank at least of third of a litre in less than half an hour. She staggered to the bathroom and returned with several bottles of pills. Jude, who was not used to alcohol, managed to drink about another third and Eloise continued to knock it back. Then they swallowed handfuls of pills together, until they were all gone.

An hour or so later, Jude awoke and ran to the toilet to vomit. He said he probably brought everything back up although he had wanted to die. As he returned to the bedroom, Eloise was lying on her back, very still and her face was covered in vomit. He thought his survival was due to their difference in size. He felt for a heartbeat and found nothing. It was late into the night and he panicked. He put on some rubber gloves, wrapped her tiny body in a blanket and carried her to her car. He placed her across the back seat and went back into the house to fetch the vodka, suicide note and an empty bottle of pills. He removed the gloves for a moment to carefully peel the label with his name from the pill container. He then went back into the house for a cloth to wipe away his fingerprints. He put the gloves back on and hurriedly drove to Epping Forest. When he reached his destination, he sat Eloise in the driver's seat and placed the bottles on her lap. He put her suicide note in the glove box and then wiped everything he had touched with the cloth just to be on the safe side. He left the key in the ignition, took the blanket and hurried away.

He stopped a couple of miles away in a secluded area where he was out of sight. He stayed there until morning, keeping himself warm under the blanket. As soon as it was light, he made his way to the train station and took himself home. He washed the blanket and disposed of all the empty bottles as soon as he arrived back at his house. Then he noticed her handbag on his bedroom floor. It was too late to take it back to her car so he burned it and all the contents in his garden brazier.

***

I will never know how much truth was in Jude's story. I can picture Eloise coerced into participating in this drama but there were too many unanswered questions. Did he actually take any tablets at all? Was it a proper suicide pact that went wrong, leaving Jude behind? He made it sound like it was her idea which he just went along with. That was the part I found hard to believe. She would never have initiated such a thing because she feared death too much. Perhaps she really had become weary of living. Jude had promised they would die together which could have finally given her courage. The tragedy was that she went alone in the end. He was alive, well and fucking me.

***

"It must have been awful, Jude."

"It was. If I'd called an ambulance or the police, I could've been banged up for life. I don't deserve that. Besides she was already dead."

Then he began to cry hard and I thought the tears would never stop.

"It's alright, Jude. It was her fault anyway – always the fucking drama queen. She didn't even have the guts to top herself without dragging you into it. There was nothing you could've done anyway."

"Don't talk about her like that. Whatever she said about me, I did love her. I've just been too scared to feel."

"I'm sorry, Jude. I've been a bit hard on her, haven't I?"

Had I gained his trust after all of our pillow-talk, or blown it by over-playing the bitch act? I felt confident, but had to move swiftly. He might easily change his mind which could place me in danger.

I rolled over and kissed him long and lovingly.

"I want more of that sublime dick and this time I'm taking charge."

He remained propped up by his pillows, looking relaxed and welcoming with his hands behind his head. I mounted his magnificent length and rode it slowly up and down. He was beautiful and radiated a majestic allure. I doubt he ever realised just how much he was loved. He could barely understand the concept and I felt sorry for him in a way. I would always remember him like this. Once again I could feel Eloise burning through me. Perhaps there was an afterlife – perhaps she needed to be there. I was inches away from the sword on his wall – the present from Eloise.

I continued to pleasure him as I stared at the weapon, and then I whispered, "You can't love can you?"

"What?" he groaned.

"Did you love Eloise?"

"YES I DID! Sorry, Pandora, we have to stop this."

He pushed me upward and awkwardly pulled me off his dick. He threw me headfirst to his side and my face almost hit the wall behind. As I rose to steady myself, the sword was within my grasp. I quickly pulled it from its hook and held it by my side. Jude remained on his back, unaware and staring at the ceiling with empty eyes. In a matter of seconds the blade had impaled through his chest. He looked at me and smiled.

"Thanks, Pandora. I can be with her now," he said quietly as blood appeared from the corner of his mouth.

How had he found strength for such drama on his deathbed – or was it real? One never knew what went on in that head of his. He began to choke and make gurgling noises. His eyes were focused on something that made him smile – but nothing was there – and that shine, so easily adopted, became brighter than ever.

He whispered, "Cathy," before his eyelids fell shut – he was dead.

I put my head on the pillow and lightly touched his angelic peaceful face. I had taken a life and was shocked by my capacity to do so with such ease. But this evil, charismatic monster could no longer search for victims and inflict pain. I felt such a sense of loss. Eloise's death hit me harder than ever. I began to sob. Perhaps there was a little tear for Jude too.

***

I had planned everything to the letter. *What if Jude's intention was to goad me into killing him anyway?* It was too easy and the mace spray had never once left my bag. From the moment he saw me, he appeared calm and without a care in the world. Now I will never know. Maybe he really did want to die and it all went wrong, so he had me put it right. Or perhaps he had no intention of taking his life and simply wanted rid of Eloise. He knew she was wise to him, even though her love was unconditional. People like Jude hate to have their insanity exposed – their victims become harder to manipulate and are no longer of use to them. Whichever way I look at it, she would still be alive if there had never been a Jude. I despised him.

I took the sword and made a light flesh wound across my throat. As I checked the cut in the bathroom mirror, I noticed some pumice on the side of the bath. I rubbed my arms and wrists until they appeared bruised and chafed. Then I rinsed, dried and returned it to the bath. I was dazed and numb as I phoned the emergency services.

Chapter 21
Aftermath and the Law

I was taken to a Sexual Assault Referral Centre, accompanied by three police officers, two of them being women. They needed to check for signs of sexual intercourse and injuries to suggest that force was used. Of course there was enough of Jude's DNA inside me to prove that sex had taken place, plus my bruises. They also gave me the morning after pill. The examinations and tests were nothing compared to what I had gone through already, so I felt no humiliation at all. The officers remained outside the doctor's room throughout my ordeal. I had killed Jude and even if my pleas of self-defence were believed, it was protocol for me to be watched over. After the physical evidence had been gathered and I was permitted to shower, I was taken to the local police station for questioning. A female detective probed me relentlessly but I felt comfortable with her – I think she believed me from the start.

"This interview will be recorded, Pandora because a death has occurred. Do you understand?"

"Yes."

She recorded a preamble before the questioning began.

"Did you kill Jude Wilkinson, Pandora?"

"Yes, but it was self defence. He raped me."

"At approximately what time did the assault take place, Pandora?"

"I think it was around 5 pm."

"What were you doing at Mr. Wilkinson's house?"

"I went to ask him if he knew why my friend had killed herself."

"What happened to your friend?"

"Her name was Eloise Fry. She died of an overdose about ten days ago."

The officer began to search on her computer.

"Why would Mr. Wilkinson know anything?"

"She left me her diaries and the last entry said she was going to see him."

"What do you mean 'left you her diaries?' There can't have been a will reading yet."

"I have a spare key to her flat and she always said her ex-husband must never see them."

"So you helped yourself to them?"

"Yes, I always promised her I would take them if anything happened to her."

"Did she think she was in danger?"

"I didn't think so at the time. She was very quirky and talked of wills and funeral arrangements for as long as I can remember."

"What else did the diaries say?"

"I don't know, I've only read the last few entries. I needed to know why she was so upset. I can't bring myself to read all of it just yet."

This was the most crucial lie of the many to follow. They would soon read the diaries and know every detail. If they knew I was aware of Jude's awful behaviour, it could affect my defence.

"Why didn't you bring the diaries to us?"

"I didn't think he'd done anything wrong at first. I thought perhaps they'd just argued or cancelled their date. I just wanted to see if he knew anything."

"Were they in a relationship, Pandora?"

"Yes, for just over a year but it was always on and off. I was the only person fully aware of it."

"Why's that?"

"She had a violent ex-husband and didn't want him finding out."

"Did Jude and Eloise argue much?"

"Yes, she was often upset but a lot of couples argue, don't they? So I didn't think much of it really."

"We will have to see these diaries, Pandora. I'll arrange for you to be driven to your house. Is that okay?"

"Yes."

"Now, let's get back to today. Can you tell me the sequence of events leading up to the assault?"

There began my bogus statement.

"I arrived at Jude's house at approximately 2.30pm with some photos of Eloise I thought he might like. We chatted for over two hours about Eloise and I asked if he knew why she'd killed herself. He claimed that they'd argued over the phone, so he cancelled their meeting and he hadn't heard from her since."

"Did you believe him?"

"No, he said he felt responsible for her death but I felt his tears and grief were a bit forced. I asked if he was sure nothing else had happened which he didn't like at all. He suddenly became angry and started shouting at me."

"What did he say?"

"He said that Eloise was a selfish bitch who gave him nothing but heartache and had tried to involve him in suicide pacts more than once. Then he admitted she was with him the day that she died and she'd overdosed in his bedroom. He knew what she was doing and just left her to it while he watched a film.

As soon a she was dead he drove her to Epping Forest and left her there. Then he took the first train at 5 am back home. He'd planted the pills, note and drink in her car but had forgotten her bag. He said he'd burned it in his back garden after he got back. There might still be some remains there."

"Why do you think he confessed to you?"

"I think by then he'd decided to kill me to save his own skin."

"What happened after that?"

"I was terrified. Now I knew he was more dangerous than I'd first thought. I tried to stay calm but he must have seen how frightened I was. He walked towards me, took me by the throat, pushed me towards his bedroom and threw me onto the bed. There was a sword on his wall which he took down and pressed toward to my throat. I felt a sting and my neck became cold with blood so I thought it best to keep quiet. He pulled off my trousers and underwear with one hand, whilst still holding the blade to my throat. Then he rested the weapon under his pillow. After that he held me down by my wrists and raped me. When he'd finished he laid back on the bed laughing."

"Jude was a strong man, Pandora. He'd overpowered and raped you, so how did you eventually manage to stab him?"

"I could see the sword handle poking out of the pillow under his head as he rested, so I took a chance and grabbed it. I had nothing to lose. He reached out to take it back and cut his hand badly. I sat up quickly and pushed my knee hard into his testicles. He said he was going to kill me so I pushed the sword into his chest."

"He actually threatened to kill you?"

"Yes, but I told you – I knew that from the start anyway. Why else would he confess?"

***

The interview concluded and I was escorted home in a surgical shirt, gown and slippers. I handed all of the journals over to the police officers, along with my passport and we returned to the station. I purposely kept the book draft under lock and key because I would need that for myself.

I was made to sleep in a cell for the night and was called back to the interview room in the morning. They had managed to read the most crucial events between the four of them. Jude's behaviour, his rape of Eloise and the final diary entry were evidence enough to set me free for the time being. I was given police bail. They told me they would keep the diaries for further investigation along with my passport. They would be returned to me after the court hearing and inquest, which would probably take place in five to six months' time. I would, of course, have to attend, but I was confident this would just be a formality where my innocence would be ascertained. I felt sure I had cracked it.

After I returned home, I felt nothing. My curtains remained drawn and I stayed inside the house. For the first few mornings, it felt as though I had woken from a nightmare, only to realise that the nightmare was real. It took me a few days to come to my senses and decide that Jude was not going to destroy me as he had Eloise.

***

Andy phoned and asked if Jude was back from his holiday.

"No, Andy, I can't seem to get hold of him. I'll ring you as soon as I hear something."

He deserved to know the truth, but not yet. It was still too soon and I had to find the right words to tell him what had happened.

After two weeks, I received a visit from the police. I still felt confident that they were happy with my statement of events. A court date had been set for mid -December. Chances were that I would be off the hook by Christmas.

* * *

As the days wore on, I was almost back to my normal self. I went shopping and did all the usual every day things. But something was wrong – I could feel it. A strange and giddy sensation often came over me as I shopped and I kept dropping things. I simply put it down to the trauma I had suffered. After another week, I decided to make an appointment with the doctor. My kitchen had also become a battlefield where I injured myself repeatedly. I had become very clumsy. Most mornings I awoke with a blinding headache and would vomit soon after. I thought it could be a form of depression, although I had never been one to suffer from that sort of thing.

Now it was time to contact Andy, so I invited him to my house. I trusted him and decided to tell him everything. He was dumbfounded.

"Are you mad?"

"I had to do it my way, Andy."

"Yes, but he could have killed you."

"Well he didn't, did he? I got in first. "

"He deserved it, Pandora."

"I know, it was him or me, but I still can't believe I've murdered someone."

"Don't you ever feel bad about it, Pandora. He was an evil bastard but you put yourself in far too much danger. I'm angry with you for that."

"He would never have confessed in front of you, Andy. I had to take my chances."

Andy stayed with me that night. All we did was hug – and for the first time in weeks, I felt good.

The next morning Andy got up early for work.

"Do you want me to come back tonight, Pandora?"

"If you want to."

I knew it was too soon after Eloise's death, but I nodded – something felt wrong and I needed Andy right now.

Epilogue

My relationship with Andy quickly developed into what I suppose you would call a love affair. Eloise had originally been our common bond and now we had found one of our own. We had leaned on each other at first, but soon he was able to make me laugh – I very much doubt anyone else could have done that. He was different to most of the men I had known. He was in touch with his feminine side which was actually very appealing. I wished Eloise had chosen him over Jude. If she had however, she would be alive today and I would be without Andy – that selfish thought made me feel terrible. Andy and I soon became almost inseparable.

He continued to badger me into showing him the journals and I repeatedly told him, "Maybe one day."

I decided to steer clear of the subject until he gave up asking. Eloise would have hated the idea. He knew the gist, so why torture himself further by reading her most intimate thoughts about Jude? Besides, I was falling for him and it would hurt watching him cry over Eloise. He took me to several hospital appointments for various tests and was extremely supportive during my time of mental and physical trauma.

A couple of days after my bail had been set, the police found the remains of a makeup compact in Jude's back garden brazier. They also found the car rug, which had been washed but still had long, fair hair woven through it. My worries lessened as I felt sure they believed my story now. They also took Jude's computer for analysis and I can only imagine they found his conversations with various women. Eloise had always known about Jude's cyber flirtations and I think she had accepted it in the end – as though it was simply a strange and harmless foible of his.

The police divulged little of their investigations and just asked me the odd question here and there, such as, "What sort of items did Eloise carry in her handbag and did I know what colour the rug was?"

I suppose they needed to be careful with certain information before the hearing. All I needed to do was to tell my story and hope the evidence would support it. They were not at liberty to put words into my mouth, but the way the officer in charge spoke to me always put me at ease. She was so sincere and the things she hinted at gave me hope. She was extremely kind and gentle every time we talked. She enquired if Eloise had been fully aware of Jude's conduct with women on the internet. We all knew that Eloise had set him up that time on Facebook as Susie, but that was the only incident mentioned in her diaries. She told me once that he was an awful flirt and had a plethora of middle-aged ladies following his Facebook page. She would laugh although I knew she hated it. This made me wonder if the police had discovered Jude was on a grooming rampage to ensnare dozens of women. They probably had more sense than Eloise however – and shied away as soon as they realised he was mad. I was also asked if I knew of a friend of Jude's named Wendy. Was Wendy another Eloise? Had she stayed the course and fallen for Jude too? Maybe he was seeing this woman and needed shot of Eloise to make room for her. Eloise had spent much less time with Jude recently after all. Wendy must have played a part or why else would the police mention her by name? Perhaps they were questioning Wendy as well. Maybe she was dead. My head was spinning.

The police informed me that Jude's body had been released for burial. His estranged brother had arranged the funeral and had also reclaimed Jude's house. It had never belonged entirely to Jude in the first place. It was the childhood family home apparently and left to all of the children, who allowed Jude to remain there after his mother's death. So his claim of buying it outright was yet another tale. I hoped his brother had taken the dogs into his care but never found out. I knew there would be nobody at the funeral except for a priest. His family had never visited him and hardly ever kept in touch, so I talked Andy into coming with me. It felt fitting in a way and I needed to see him gone for good – to make sure he was actually dead – although, of course, I knew he was. I convinced Andy that it was the correct thing to do. I was right; there were no mourners, not even any mysterious women. It was a warm and sunny day, and I felt Eloise had been cheated by the clouds and rain when she was laid to rest. As I watched Jude's coffin being lowered into the ground, I threw a handful of dry soil after it. I felt liberated by the finality of the gesture – his murderer had performed this traditional symbol of love and grief. The corner of my mouth lifted into a small, satisfied smile. His madness had always putrefied everything around him and now he was stuck in the dirt.

Jude forever complained that he was unloved, yet all he ever did was drive people away. I wanted to know more, but probably never would – I was running out of time. I read all I could about the traits of psychopaths, sociopaths and narcissists and he fitted the profiles for them all. It was confusing because I was certain he had felt something for Eloise, although these people seemingly have no room for emotional attachment. They only victimise, manipulate and perform to get what they want. They crave love and attention but can never return it – they have no capacity for love. Jude had always talked of his love for dogs and other animals which was another atypical trait that stumped me. I wondered if he was cruel to them in private. His grandiose ideas about himself were another sign of these disorders – and his were completely off the wall.

I began to read one of his children's books which he stated were based on his childhood with a bit of fantasy thrown in. The little boy in the book was from another planet and destined to rule the world which was very telling and, frankly, rather frightening. I believe he seriously wanted to rule the world. He was so very charming and witty and could beguile a room full of people easily. He had lived on the edge for most of his life until it became too dangerous – too many people were wise to him. He became contemptuous of those who learned what he was, even if they understood and genuinely wanted to help – like Eloise. He lacked the intelligence he believed he possessed however, and formed very few relationships, even in the short term. Then along came the internet. What a wonderful opportunity for him to con and connive. He could keep people hanging at a safe distance with a view to future enslavement. There was never any remorse, just lies, games and a deluded mission that sucked the life out of anyone who was stupid enough to put up with him.

Soon Andy and I had found our own ground. We were of similar age, laughed at the same jokes and enjoyed the same kind of music. We ate out regularly and both loved a good drink.

The saddest thing for me was that Eloise never even got to see her book in print. She died shortly before the publishing date and Frank told the publisher to go ahead – rubbing his greedy hands, no doubt. But at least her wish was fulfilled.

***

The story of Eloise and Jude was intended for publication. I knew that as soon as I read the draft I had kept hidden. It read in a very professional manner as opposed to a bunch of illegible scribbles. Eloise always thought she would meet an early death. It was strange how I had no foreboding of my own fate. Most of her book was identical to her somewhat sketchier diary entries. She had obviously intended for it to be released in such a form. I contacted Eloise's publisher, telling her that another book was on its way. I warned it could take a while, as I was attempting to give it some of my own input and finish it myself. She told me she would be happy to take a look at it.

So this is the story of Eloise and Jude. I have attempted to put it together with some of my own words to the best of my ability – with the true ending – not the happy one Eloise had hoped for. Any discrepancies can be with dealt with by Eloise's publisher. I have left the manuscript in the capable hands of my solicitor with strict instructions for it to remain sealed until after my death, or at the point of my dementia – whichever comes first. I have been diagnosed with an aggressive, inoperable brain tumour and have around five months left to live. If I last those months, I will begin to lose my faculties towards the end, or I could have a seizure and die quite suddenly according to my doctor. I have asked my solicitor to pass this book onto the publisher and for all royalties to be paid to Charlie. Soon Frank, Charlie and the world will know the truth. They will know it was Jude whom Eloise met on her birthday. They will know exactly what Jude told me and how I lied to save myself. Even Andy will learn more of the facts I have kept from him. They can interpret events and make up their own minds how they see fit. Jude's murder will become a cold case which should keep the authorities busy for a while. At least I duped them and will probably be dead before it comes to court. I am sure Frank will survive with life, although I worry about Charlie. His father was a dreadful influence but Charlie is young and impressionable. I am sure that he misses his mum.

I will never find out who Wendy was but I am convinced she was Jude's latest conquest. He needed people to admire and worship him. Eloise knew too much. Perhaps Wendy was another gullible besotted woman like Eloise and I have saved her – I do hope so.

Andy is taking me travelling across Europe whilst I still have the capacity to enjoy it. I feel okay, apart from my early morning headache and the odd dizzy spell. Andy is my rock and has had more than his fair share of heartache. I refuse to spend my final months in a prison or some awful institution.

I have felt nothing but hatred for Jude these past months but now my life is limited, my emotions are changing. I am trying to make sense of things and some sort of peace with the world. I forgive my mother for being a nightmare and forgive Eloise for being so foolish. I am even trying to forgive Jude, which is by far the hardest task. It is important to remind myself that Jude suffered a mental health condition. He was traumatised as a child – that much was true. I still think he probably loved Eloise in a certain twisted way that overwhelmed him with panic. But she deserved better. If only they had learned to really love themselves first – the outcome could have been very different. Perhaps we are more than worm fodder. I hope there is a heaven after all. Not just for myself but for Eloise and even Jude – though I still think I am being far too generous with him. Maybe things are different there – like going home and losing all our earthly stupidity, sickness and pain. It would also be nice if we could choose our favourite age and stay that way forever. I would like to be around thirty and you can bet Eloise would want to be nineteen again. Perhaps Jude is a decent fellow and is making Eloise happy now. Maybe I will see them again and everything will have been put right. I doubt it though – but after all the mess that has gone before – it is a lovely thought!

Contacts

Email : cjlockwood56@googlemail.com

Website : http://cjlockwood56.wix.com/catherine-lockwood-

Facebook : https://www.facebook.com/maxchan68?fref=ts

Parts of this story are based on real-life events. I hope you enjoyed it. There is much help online for victims of sociopaths and narcissists. There are many sites and fora which can easily be found via Google. Visit:

https://www.facebook.com/groups/889924227700680/?fref=ts

***

www.ingramcontent.com/pod-product-compliance
Lightning Source LLC
Chambersburg PA
CBHW060624290526
45793CB00001B/125